Harry Stillwell Edwards

His defense

And other stories

Harry Stillwell Edwards

His defense
And other stories

ISBN/EAN: 9783742891532

Manufactured in Europe, USA, Canada, Australia, Japa

Cover: Foto ©Thomas Meinert / pixelio.de

Manufactured and distributed by brebook publishing software
(www.brebook.com)

Harry Stillwell Edwards

His defense

HIS DEFENSE

AND OTHER STORIES

BY

HARRY STILLWELL EDWARDS

Author of " Two Runaways and Other Stories "

NEW YORK

THE CENTURY CO.

1899

CONTENTS

v

LIST OF ILLUSTRATIONS

vii

HIS DEFENSE

HIS DEFENSE

I

"WHAT?"

Colonel Rutherford shot a swift glance from the brief he was examining at the odd figure before him, and resumed his occupation quickly, to hide the smile that was already lifting the heavy frown from his face. "Indicted for what?"

"For the cussin' of my mother-in-law; an' I want you ter be on hand at court ter make er speech for me when hit comes up."

"Did you cuss her?"

The lawyer fell easily into the vernacular of his visitor, but he was afraid to lift his eyes again higher than the tips of his own polished boots, resting upon the table in front of him, in the good old Georgia fashion.

"Did I?" The stranger shifted his hat to the other hand and wiped his brow with a cotton handkerchief. His voice was low and plaintive. "I sho'ly did cuss. I cussed 'er comin' an' goin', for'ards and back'ards, all erroun' an' straight through. Ain't no use ter deny hit. I done hit."

He was tall, and in old age would be gaunt. He was also sunburned, and stooped a little, as from hard labor and long walking in plowed ground or long riding behind slow mules. One need not have been a physiognomist to discover that, although yet young, the storms of life had raged about him. But the lawyer noticed that he was neat, and that his jeans suit was home-made, and his pathetic homespun shirt and sewed-on collar — the shirt and collar that never will sit right for any country housewife, however devoted —were ornamented with a black cravat made of a ribbon and tied like a school-girl's sash.

The defendant leaned over the table as he finished speaking, resting his hands thereon, and thrusting forward his aquiline features, shame and excitement struggling for expression in his blue eyes.

"Did she cuss you first?"

The stranger looked surprised.

"No."

"Did she abuse you, strike you, insult you — did she ever chuck anything at you?"

"Why, no! — you see, hit was n't edzactly the words —"

"Then it seems to me, my friend, that you have no use for a lawyer. I never take any kind of a criminal case for less than one hundred dollars, and the court will hardly fine you that much if you plead guilty. By your own statement, you see, you are guilty, and I can't help you. Better go and plead guilty and file an exculpatory affidavit—"

"No, sir. That 'll do for some folks, but not for me. I never dodged in my life, and I ain't goin' ter dodge now. All you got ter do is ter make er speech. I want you ter tell them for me—"

"But what is the use, my friend? Can't you see—"

"Don't make no difference. You go. I 'll be thar with your money."

"All right," was the laughing rejoinder; "but you are simply wasting time and money."

"That 's my business. No man ever wasted his time or money when he was settin' himself right before his folks."

Lifting his head with an air the memory of which dwelt with the attorney for many a day, the novel client departed, leaving him still laughing. He opened his docket and wrote, in the absence of further information: "The man who cussed his mother-in-law, Crawford Court, $100."

Court opened in Crawford County as usual. The city lawyers followed the judge over from Macon in nondescript vehicles, their journey enlivened by many a gay jest and well-told tale, to say nothing of refreshments by the way. The autumn woods were

glorious in the·year's grand sunset. Like masque-
raders in some wild carnival, the gums and sumacs
and hickories and persimmons and maples mingled
their flaunting banners and lifted them against the
blue and cloudless skies. Belated cotton-pickers stole
the last of the fields' white lint, and sang in harmonies
that echoed from the woodlands, seeming to voice the
gladness of unseen revelers.

And Knoxville, waking from its dull dreams, took
on life and color for the week. Horses tugged at the
down-sweeping limbs or dozed contentedly beside the
racks; and groups of country folks, white and black,
discussed solemnly or with loud jest the ever-chang-
ing situation. The session of court, brief though it
be, is fraught with meaning for many families, the
chief points of friction being the issues between land-
lord and tenant, factor and farmer, loan associations
and delinquent debtors. And there is always the
criminal side of court, with its sable fringe of evil-
doers.

The sheriff, in obedience to time-honored custom,
had shouted from the front steps the names of all
parties concerned in the case of the State *versus* Hiram
Ard, and the State, through its urbane solicitor, the
Hon. Jefferson Brown, had announced " Ready," when
Colonel Rutherford felt a hand upon his shoulder,
and, looking up, saw a half-familiar face earnestly
bent toward his own.

"Hit 's come," said the stranger, his blue eyes full of excitement; "an' thar 's your hunderd."

"Beg your pardon," said the lawyer; "some mistake! I — don't think — I can exactly locate you."

"What? I'm the man they say that cussed his mother-in-law!"

"Why, of course, of course! One moment, your Honor, until I can consult my client."

The consultation was brief. The lawyer urged a plea of guilty. The client was determined to go to trial.

"Ready for the defense!" said Colonel Rutherford, in despair, waving his client to his seat with a gesture that seemed to disclaim responsibility for anything that might happen.

The usual preliminaries and formalities were soon disposed of, and the jury stricken, twelve good men and true, as their names will show; for to adjudge this case were assembled there Dike Sisson, Bobby Lewis, Zeke Cothern, Tony Hutt, Hob Garrett, Jack Dermedy, Tommie Liptrot, Jack Doozenbery, Abe Ledzetter, Cran Herringdine, Bunk Durden, and Tim Newberry.

The State, upon this occasion, had but one witness. Mrs. Jessy Gonder was called to the stand. The lady was mild-looking and thin, and something in her bearing unconsciously referred one to a happier past. But the good impression — perhaps it is

better to say the soft impression — vanished when
she loosened her bonnet-strings and tongue, and
with relentless, drooping mouth corners — those
dead smiles of bygone days — began to relate her
grievance.

Well, Mrs. Gonder was one of those unfortunate
women whom adversity sours and time cannot
sweeten; and that is all there is of it. In sharp,
crisp tones and bitter words she told of her experience with the defendant. The narrative covered
years of bitterness, disappointment, wounded vanity,
and hatred, and was remarkable for its excess of
feeling. It was, from a professional standpoint, over-
done. It was an outburst. Members of the admir-
able jury who had looked with surprise and animosity
upon Hiram Ard began to regard him with something like sympathy; for, disguise it as she might, it
was plain to all men that the overwhelming cause
of her grievance was Hiram's conquest of her only
daughter. Bobby Lewis leaned over and whispered
to Bunk Durden, and both young men laughed until
their neighboring jurors were visibly affected, and
the court knocked gently with its gavel. When she
came to the cause of war wherein this low-bred son-
in-law had cursed around her,— her, Jessy Gonder,—
had entered the house she occupied and had forcibly
taken away a sewing-machine loaned by her own
daughter, her voice trembled and she shook her

clenched fist above the rail, her eyes, the while, fairly blazing in the shadow of her black bonnet. She sank back at last, exhausted.

While the witness was testifying the defendant looked straight ahead of him, settling slowly in his seat, until his matched hands, supported by his elbows that rested upon the chair, almost covered his face. From time to time a wave of color flushed his cheeks and brow. Then he seemed to wander off to scenes the woman's words recalled, and he became oblivious to his surroundings. When at last his attorney touched him and called him to the witness-stand, he started violently, and with difficulty regained his composure.

"Tell the jury what you know of this case," said Rutherford; and then to the court: "This seems to be purely a family quarrel, your Honor, and I trust the defendant will be allowed to proceed without interruption of any kind. Go on, sir," he concluded, to the latter.

The defendant seated himself in the witness-stand, his arm on the rail, and said:

"Hit's er long story, my friends, an' if thar war n't nothin' in the case but er fine I would n't take your time. But thar 's er heap more, an' ef you 'll all hear me out, I don't think any of you 'll believe I 'm much ter be blamed. So far as the cussin' is concerned, thar ain't no dispute erbout that. I done hit, an' I ought n't

er done hit. No gentleman can cuss erroun' er woman,
an' for the first time in my life I war n't er gentleman.
I could er come here an' pleaded guilty an' quit, but
that don't square er gentleman's record. I hired er
lawyer ter take my case, an' did hit ter have him put me
up here where I could get er chance ter face my people,
an' say I was wrong, an' sorry for hit, an' willin' ter take
the consequences. That 's the kind of man Hiram
Ard is."

All the shamefacedness was gone from the man.
He had straightened up in his chair, and his blue eyes
were beaming with earnestness. His declaration,
simple and direct, had penetrated every corner of the
room. In a moment he had caught the attention of
the crowd, for all the world loves a manly man, and
from that moment their attention never wavered.

"But," he continued, when the silence had become
intense, "I ain't willin' for you ter think that Hiram
Ard could cuss erroun' any woman offhand an' for er
little matter.

"Some of you knowed me when I was er barefooted
boy, with no frien' in the worl' 'ceptin' ma an' pa,
an' not them long. This trouble started away back
thar — when I was that kind er boy an' goin' ter
school. I was 'mos' too big ter go ter school, an' she —
I mean Cooney, Cooney Gonder — was 'mos' too young.
Somehow I got ter sorter lookin' out for her on the
road, gentlemen, an' totin' her books, an' holdin' her

steady crossin' the logs over Tobysofkee Creek an'
the branches. An' at school, when the boys teased
her an' pulled her hair an' hid her dinner-bucket, I
sorter tuk up for her; an' the worst fight I ever had
was erbout Cooney Gonder.

"Well, so it went on year in an' out. Then pa died,
an' the ole home was sold for his debts. An' then ma
died. All I had left, gentlemen, was erbout sixty
acres on Tobysofkee an' thirty up in Coldneck dees-
tric'; an' not er acre cleared. But I went ter work.
I cut down trees an' made er clearin', an' I hired er
mule an' planted er little crop. Cotton fetched er big
price that year, an' I bought the mule outright. An'
then er feller come erlong with er travelin' sawmill,
an' I let him saw on halves ter get lumber ter build
my house. Hit was just er two-room house, but hit
war mine, an' I was the proudes'! I bought ernother
mule on credit, an' the new lan' paid for hit too an'
lef' me money besides. An' then I put on ernother
room.

"Well, all this time I was tryin' ter keep comp'ny
with Cooney, gentlemen — I say tryin', 'cause her
folks did n't think much of me. My family war n't
much, an' Cooney's was good blood an' er little stuck-
up. An' Cooney — well, Cooney had done growed ter
be the prettiest an' sweetest in all the Warrior dees-
tric', as you know, an' they had done made her er
teacher, for she was smart as she was pretty. An'

she was good—too good for me. Ter this day I don't
understan' hit. Cooney say hit was because I was
honest an' er man all over; that was the excuse she
gave for lovin' me. But I do know that when she
said yes, two things happened: I kissed her, an'
there was er riot in Cooney's family. Cooney's ma
was the last ter come roun', an' I don't think she ever
did quite come roun', for she war n't at the wedding;
but, so help me God, I never bore her no ill will.
Hit must have been hard ter give Cooney up.

"I will never forget the day, gentlemen, she come
into that little home. Hit was like bein' born ag'in; I
was that happy. I made the po'est crop I ever made
in my life; but, bless you, the whole place changed.
Little vines come up an' made er shade on the po'ch,
an' flowers growed about the yard in places that look
like they had been waitin' for flowers always. An'
the little fixin's on the bureau and windows, an' white
stuff hangin' ter the mantelpieces — well, I never
knowed what hit was ter live before.

"Then at last I went ter work. It was four mules
then, an' me in debt for two, an' some rented land;
but no man who had Cooney could honestly call himself in debt. I worked day in an' out, rain or shine,
hot or cold, an' I struck hit right. Cooney was sewin'
for two an' sewin' on little white things for another,
and we were the happiest. One day I come home 'fo'
dark ter find Cooney was gone ter her neighbor's. I

slipped in on her, an' thar she was er-sewin' on er sewin'-machine, an' proud of the work as I was of the first land I ever laid off. Hit was hard ter pull her away. Well, I did n't say nothin'; I thought, an' I kept hit all ter myself. I went ter town that fall with my cotton, an' when I had done paid my draft at the warehouse I had seventy dollars left. What did I do with hit? What do you reckon I did with hit?"

The aquiline face took on a positively beautiful smile. The speaker leaned over the rail and talked confidentially to the jury.

"Well, here 's what I did, gentlemen. I went ter whar that one-arm old soldier stays what keeps sewin'-machines an' the tax-books, an' I planked down sixty of my pile for one of them. An' then I went home an' set the thing in the settin'-room while Cooney was gettin' supper; an' I let her eat, but I could n't hardly swaller, I was so full of that machine."

He laughed aloud at this point, and several of the jury joined him. The court smiled and lifted a law-book in front of his face.

"When I took her in thar an' turned up the light, Cooney like ter fainted. 'My wife don't have ter sew on no borrowed machine no more,' says I, just so; an' she fell ter cryin' an' huggin' me; an' by an' by we got down ter work. I 'll be doggoned if we did n't set up tell one er'clock playin' on that thing! She 'd sew, an' then I 'd sew, an' then I 'd run the wheel under-

neath an' she 'd run the upper works. We hemmed
and hawed all the napkins over, an' the table-cloths;
an' tucked all the pillow frills; an' Cooney made me
er handkerchief out of something. Gentlemen, next
ter gettin' Cooney, hit was the happiest night of my
life ! "

II

Hiram paused to take breath, and the tension on the audience being relieved, they moved, looked into one another's faces, and, smiling, exchanged comments. A breath of spring seemed to have invaded the autumn.

"Would n't believe he was guilty ef he swore hit," said a voice somewhere, and there was applause, which was promptly suppressed. Hiram did not hear the comment. He was lost in his dream.

"Then the baby come. But before he come I saw Cooney begin ter change. She 'd sit an' droop, an' brighten up an' droop erg'in, lookin' away off; an' her step got slow. Then, one day, hit come ter me: she was homesick for her ma. Well, gentlemen, I reck'n 't was natchul at that time. She never had said nothin', but the way her ma had done an' the way she had talked about me was the grief of her life. She could n't see how she was goin' ter meet the new trouble erlone. I fixed hit for her. I took her out on the po'ch where she could break down without my seemin' ter know hit, an' I tole her as how hit did look like hit was a shame for her ma ter have ter live off at

13

her sister's, an' her own chile keepin' house, with a
comp'ny room; an' I believed I 'd drive over an' tell
her ter let bygones be bygones, an' come an' live with
us; that I did n't set no store by the hard things she 'd
said, an' we would do our best for her. Well, that
got Cooney. She dropped her head down in my lap,
an' I knowed I 'd done hit the nail on the head.
Natchully I was happy erlong with her.

"Well, I went an' made my best talk, an' when I
got done, gentlemen, what you reck'n Cooney's ma
said — what do you reck'n? She said: 'How 's
Cooney?' 'Po'ly,' says I. 'I thought so,' says she,
'er you would n't er come.' I 'll get my things an'
go.' But Cooney was so happy when she did come, I
caught the fever too, an' thought me an' the old lady
would get on all right at last. But we did n't.
Seemed like pretty soon ma begin ter look for things
ter meddle in, an' she got er new name for me ev'y
time I come erroun'. I did n't answer back, because
she was Cooney's ma. I grit my teeth an' went on.
But she 'd come out an' lean on the fence, even, when
I was plowin', an' talk. 'Look like any fool,' she said
one day, 'look like any fool would know better 'n ter
lay off land with er twister. Why n't yer git er roun'
p'inted shovel?' My lan' was new, gentlemen, an' full
of roots; that 's why.

"An' she 'd look at my hogs an' say: 'I allus did
despise Berkshires. Never saw er sow that would n't

eat pigs after er while. Why n't you cross 'em on the
big Guinea ?' An' then, the chickens. 'Thar's them
Wyandottes! Never knew one ter raise er brood yet;
an' one rooster takes more pasture than er mule.' An'
I paid ten dollars for three, gentlemen. An' then,
Cooney's mornin'-glories made her sick. An' she
did n't like sewin'-machines; they made folks want
more clothes than they ought ter have, an' made the
wash too big. An' what she called 'jimcracks' was
Cooney's pretties in the sittin'-room.

"But I stood it; she was Cooney's ma. Only, when
the mockin'-bird's cage door was found opened an' he
gone, I like to have turned my mind loose, for I had
my suspicions, an' have yet. He was a little bird
when I found him. I was clearin' my lan', an' one of
these new niggers come erlong with er single-barrel
gun, an' shot both the old birds right before my eyes
with one load. I was that mad I took up er loose
root an' frailed him tell he could n't walk straight,
an' I bent the gun roun' er tree an' flung hit after
him. Then I went ter the nest in the haw-bush, an'
started out ter raise the four young ones. I could n't
find er bug ter save me, though it looked easy for the
old birds, so I took them home an' tried eggs an'
potato. Well, one by one they died, until but one
was left. When Cooney come he was grown, an' with
the dash of white on his wings all singers have. But
he never would sing — I think he was lonesome. The

first night she come, I woke ter hear the little feller
singin' away like his heart was too full ter hold hit all.
I turned over ter wake Cooney, that she might hear
him too, an' what do you reck'n? The moonlight had
found er way in through the half-open blinds an' had
fell across her face. Hit shone out there in the dark-
ness like an angel's, an' that little lonesome bird had
seen hit for the first time. Hit started the song in him
just like hit had in me, an' God knows—" His voice
quivered a moment and he looked away, a slight gesture supplying a conclusion.

"Then the baby come, an' when Cooney said, 'We'll
name hit Jessy, after ma,' I said, 'Good enough,
Cooney. Hit's natchul.'

"Looks like that ought ter have made it easier all
erroun', but hit did n't. Hit all got worse. An' ter keep
the peace, I got not ter comin' inter the house tell the
dinner-bell would ring. I'd jus' set on the fence,
pretendin' I was er-watchin' the stock feed. An' after
dinner I'd go out erg'in an' set on the fence ter keep
the peace. Not that I blamed Cooney's ma so much,
for I did n't. Nobody ever said hit for her but me, an'
I don't mind sayin' hit now: but she has had trouble
ernough for four women; an' her boy died. He was
er good boy, if thar ever was one. I remember the
time we went ter school together; an' when he died of
the fever, why, hit was then I sorter took his place an'
looked out for Cooney all the time. Her boy died,

an' I think er heap er 'lowance ought ter be made for er widow when her boy is buried, for I don't believe there is much else left for her in this world."

The stillness in the room was absolute when the witness paused a moment, and for some reason studied his fingers, his face bent down. All eyes were unconsciously turned then toward the prosecutrix. She had moved uncomfortably many times during this narrative, and now lowered her veil, as if she felt the focus of their attention. Afterward she did not look up again. Hiram, whose face had grown singularly tender, raised his eyes, somewhat wearily, at last.

"I know what hit is to lose a child," he said gently, "for I lost Jessy. The fever came; she faded out, an'—well—we jus' put her ter sleep out under the two cedars I had left in the corner of the yard. Then hit was worse than ever, for I had Cooney ter comfort, my own load ter tote, an'—Cooney's ma was harder ter stan' than before. I studied an' studied, an' then I took Cooney out with me ter the field an' tole her what was on my mind. 'Let 's go up ter Coldneck,' says I, 'an' build us a little house jus' like the one we started with, an' plant mornin'-glories on the po'ch, an' begin over. Let 's give ma this place for life, an' two mules, an' split up. An' let 's do hit quick, 'cause I can't hold out much longer.' You see, I was

2

'fraid er myself. Well, Cooney hugged me, an' I saw
her heart was happy over the change.

"So we went. Her ma said we were fools, an'
settled down ter run her end of the bargain. An'
I 'm boun' ter say she made good crops, an', with her
nephew ter help her, got erlong well tell he married
an' went ter his wife's folks.

"Hit looked like hit was goin' ter be easy, gentlemen,
leavin' the little home; an' hit was tell Cooney got in
the wagon an' looked back — not at the house, an'
the flowers she had planted, an' the white curtains in
her winders, but at the two little cedars where Jess
was sleepin', an' the mockin'-bird balancin' an' singin'
on the highest limb. Hit was easy tell then. Her
heart jus' broke, an' she cried out ter herself: 'Ma!
ma! I would n't er treated you that-er-way — I
would n't er done hit!'" He pointed his finger at
the prosecutrix. "She did n't know Cooney felt that-
er-way, gentlemen; this is the first time. An' she
did n't know that when I came back from Macon,
next fall, an' brought er little marble slab with Jess's
name on hit, an' put hit up under the cedars, I got one
with her Tom's name on hit, too, an' went ter her ole
home, an' cleared away the weeds, an' put hit over
Tom's grave. He was er good boy — an' he was
Cooney's brother.

"Well," continued the defendant, after a pause,
"we did well. I cleared the land an' made er good

crop. An' then our own little Tom come. That 's
what we named him. An' one day Cooney asked me
ter go back an' get her sewin'-machine from her ma's.
Hit was the first plantin' day we had had in April,
an' I hated mightily ter lose er day; but Cooney never
had asked me for many things, so I went. When I
rode up, ma come out, an', restin' her hands on her
sides, she said: 'I did give you credit for some sense!
What you doin' here, an' hit the first cotton-plantin'
day of the year? I 'll be boun' you picked out this
day ter come for that ar sewin'-machine.' I tole her I
had; an' then she answered back: 'Nobody but er
natchul-born fool would come for er sewin'-machine
in that sort er wagon. You can't get hit. Thar
would n't be er whole j'int in hit when you got back!'
Well, seein' as how I had brought the thing from
Macon once in the same wagon, hit did look unrea-
sonable I could n't take hit further. But the road ter
Coldneck was rougher, an' I could n't give her no
hold on me, so back I went, twelve miles, an' er whole
day sp'iled. But Cooney was sorry, I could see; an'
she never did ask me for many things, so I borrowed
Buck Drawhorn's spring-wagon, an' next day, bright
an' early, I put out erg'in. When I got back ter the
ole home, she was stan'in' jus' like I left her, with
her hands on her sides. I did n't get time ter put in
'fo' she called out: 'Nobody but er natchul-born fool
would come here for er machine, an' clouds er-risin'

in the rain quarter. Don't you know ef that machine
gets wet hit won't be worth hits weight in ole iron?
You can't git hit!' Well, gentlemen, seems ter me
that with all our kiver mos' still in the house, she
might er loant me some ter put on that machine; but
she did n't; an' bein' 'fraid er myself, I wheeled
roun' an' went back them twelve miles erg'in. Ernother day sp'iled, an' no machine. An' I won't do
nobody er injustice, gentlemen. Hit did rain like
all-fire, though whar hit come from I don't know tell
now, an' I got wet ter the bones.

"But I was determ' then ter git that machine, if I
did n't never plant er cotton-seed. Next day I rode up
bright an' early, an' thar she was. I had n't got out
the wagon 'fo' she opened: 'You can't git that machine! You go back an' tell Cooney I 'm er-sewin'
for Hester Bloodsworth, an' when I git done I 'll let
her know. An' don't you come back here no more
tell I let you know!' Well, gentlemen, then I knowed
I had n't been 'fraid of myself for nothin'. I started
ter cussin'! I cussed all the way up the walk, an' up
the steps, an' inter the room, an' while I was shoulder-
in' that ar machine, an' while I was er-totin' hit out,
an' while I was er-loadin' hit in the wagon, an' while
I was er-drivin' off. An' when I thought of them
seventy-odd miles, an' the three days' plantin' I 'd done
lost, I stopped at the rise in the road an' cussed back
erg'in. I did hit, an', as I said, hit was ongentlemanly,

an' I 'm sorry. The only excuse I 've got, gentlemen, is I did hit in self-defense, for if I had n't cussed, so help me God, I 'd er busted wide open then an' thar ! "

The sensation that followed this remarkable climax was not soon stilled; but when quiet was at length restored, everybody's attention was attracted to the prosecutrix. She had never lifted her face from the time the defendant had mentioned the dead boy. She was still sitting with her face concealed, lost in thought, and it is likely that she never knew the conclusion of the defendant's statement. She looked up at last, impressed by the silence, and seeing the court gazing toward her as he fingered his books, she arose wearily and unsteadily.

"Can I say a few words, judge ? " Her voice was just audible at first. He nodded gravely. " Then I want to say that — I have — probably been wrong — all the way through. I have had — many troubles — many disappointments. Cooney's husband has been a good husband to her, and has always treated me kindly. I don't believe he intended to curse me, and I think if you will let me take it all back — " She hesitated and faltered.

" Be seated, madam," said the court, with something like tenderness in his voice. "Gentlemen of the jury, this case is dismissed."

The defendant came down from the stand, and paused before the woman in black a moment. Then he bent over her, but the only words any one caught were "Cooney" and "little Tom." He patted her shoulder with his rough, sunburnt hand. She hesitated a moment. and then, drawing down her veil, she took his arm and in silence left the court-room. There was a sudden burst of applause, followed by the sound of the judge's gavel. At the door, Colonel Rutherford, leaning over the rail which separated the bar from the audience, thrust something into Hiram Ard's hand. "The fee goes with the speech," he said, smiling. "Keep it for little Tom."

WILLIAM MARSDAL'S
AWAKENING

I

IT was eight o'clock in the morning; Cæsar was sweeping the broad porch of the Marsdal mansion, his gray head and wrinkled black face occasionally visible through gaps in the tall oleanders that spread their pink panicles against the whiteness of Ionic columns. It was a vision familiar to many of the passers-by; for so, in the freshness of morn, had he swept it, when not traveling with his master, for more than forty years. He had reached the end where climbed an immense Lamarque, and was shaking his broom free of dust, when the slender Moorish gate at the street entrance, a hundred feet away, clicked and closed beneath its arch, and the quick footsteps of a child were heard upon the brick walk leading to the short flight of stone steps. There is character in every footstep, and there was decided character in the crisp, clear echoes of these little heels. Ere they had reached the steps Cæsar had transferred himself to the landing, and was holding up his hands, his earnest face wearing an anxious look, and his puckered lips giving forth a series of mysterious sounds intended to attract attention and bring about silence. The owner of the little heels, however, was placidly indifferent to the pantomime. They hit brick and stone with undiminished force until she neared him. Moreover, she called to him in a clear, silvery voice, not the least modulated, "Where is Uncle William?"

The negro was in despair. "For de Lord' *sake*, honey, *ain't* you *see* me makin' *signs* for you ter stop er-comin' so hard —"

"Where is Uncle William?"

"— an' hesh yo' loud talkin'? Er runaway horse would er shied roun' de house fum me —"

"Where is Uncle William?"

— "an' you ain't so much as break yo' pace!"

"Where is Uncle William?"

"He in dere *tryin'* ter *sleep* in es *chair*," the old man continued petulantly—"*tryin'* ter snatch des er *nap* 'fo' bre'kfus'; an' you mus' n' 'sturb him, nuther!" As the little girl laughed and passed on he raised his voice: "Don't you do hit, honey! 'Deed, an' if he don't get some sleep, I don't know what 's goin' ter happen!"

"Cæsar!" The tones of a quick, harsh voice floated out.

"Yes, sah! I 'm er-comin'! Now, chile, you see

what comes of trottin' so hard on dem bricks, an' not payin' no 'tention."

"Cæsar, what the thunder are you talking about?" said the voice, testily. "Come off that porch and —"

The sentence was suspended. The owner stood in the hall. He was tall, heavy, florid, and clean-shaven; his thin, grayish-blond hair was scattered carelessly over his round head and gently waving in the draft. He was without coat or vest, his shirt was unbuttoned at the throat, and he wore slippers. The frown disappeared as he beheld his visitor, and a hearty, cheery note came into his voice.

"Ha, Humming-bird! Come in, come in! Why, God bless me, child, did Cæsar dare halt an angel upon *my* threshold? Cæsar, you black rascal!" But Cæsar had gone a roundabout way through the shrubbery to sweep off the carriage-step, and for the moment was not visible. The gentleman thereupon lifted the child in his arms and kissed her. He looked into her eyes, and then quickly toward the sky. "Bless me!" he cried again, "you are wearing your blue eyes this morning! How becoming!"

The child laughed and struggled down to the floor. She clasped something in her hand, and went into the sitting-room without ceremony.

"I'm going to make the birds sing," she said, with a precision of language unusual with Southern children, and exquisitely funny to her host.

"Oh, you are," he said, imitating her walk and tones as he followed. "Then I am coming to hear the birds sing. Silence!" he commanded, frowning around him upon the heavy furniture. "Silence while the birds sing!" And everything obeyed — everything except the gilt clock under its tall glass cover on the mantel.

The little girl climbed into a big leather chair, and seated herself upon the edge of the center-table.

"Won't you try the chandelier?" he suggested. "Birds like high places."

But she was busy with the something she had been tightly clasping in her hand, and which proved to be a curious little silver toy, half bird, half whistle, partly filled with water. Blowing into this gravely, her eyes meantime watching his face for signs of delight, she produced a series of bird-like notes and trills. He dropped into the chair at her feet.

"And what," he said, with voice husky from the intensity of his interest, and with mouth corners drawn down, "what bird in this world can sing as beau-u-u-tifully as that?"

She looked steadily at him and reflected.

"That's a mocking-bird!" she said at last.

"Oh, yes; so it is. How well you do it!"

She tried again, looking to him for approval.

"Seems like I have heard that song somewhere!"

he mused, rubbing his red ear. "Where could it have been? Surely —"

"That 's a canary," she declared. Again she essayed her skill.

He clapped his hands. "Lovely! lovely! You beat them all! But stay; what bird sings now?"

Her bird-lore was limited. She reflected again.

"Oh, that 's a parrot!"

And this time he really laughed. "It is so natural! I 'll have to give you a cracker. Polly, have a cracker?"

She pushed away his hand, and went on with her concert.

"That is my little dog barking at night," she said, in explanation.

"Good! How does he bark in the daytime?"

She showed him. It was very much like his night bark. And again her auditor laughed.

"Listen to the dog's bark," he said to the furniture.

Then the little girl from across the street gave him the cow's moo, the little calf's appeal for milk, and the hen's cackle, waiting each time for applause. Presently she remembered the circus menagerie, and she gave him, one by one, all the songs, from the elephant's down. They all sang like the mocking-bird — a discovery that filled him with a huge delight.

"I see now," he said gaily to the furniture, "how great an artist the mocking-bird really is."

And the concert went on.

Cæsar had not returned. He was outside the gate, broom in hand, talking. A lady had come leisurely along the shaded walk for the morning air, and was turning back at the Marsdal mansion, where the level land fell away abruptly, when Cæsar's profound salutation claimed her attention. It was but natural that, having inquired kindly as to the old servitor's health, she should inquire as to her neighbor, his master, and linger indulgently while he poured forth his voluble reply:

"Des toler'ble, Miss Helen — des toler'ble! When er man don't sleep, somep'n' is out er fix; an' Marse William ain't sleep er wink in er week — not er wink!"

"Is it possible?"

"Yes, ma'am. He orter be asleep right dis minute, an' I 'spec' he would, but de little gyurl fum 'cross de street come in ter blow her whistle for 'im, an' he got ter set up an' hear hit."

"Blow a whistle for him!"

"Yes, ma'am"; and Cæsar stopped to laugh. "Chile sorter got erway wid Marse William yestiddy; she sho' did. Dey come 'long hyah, er whole passel of 'em, an' tore up an' down de yard an' thoo de house like dey allus doin', an' Marse William tell 'em, if dey don't break down none of his rose-bushes, dey can ketch all de hummin'-birds dey want. He been tellin' 'em dat for twenty years, an' his ma befo' 'im."

" I remember that she used to tell me that," said the lady, smiling. " There was a tree on the other side of the house, in the grove, that attracted humming-birds. They seemed to gather something from the bark and twigs — no one could ever discover what."

" Hit 's dere yet, ma'am, de same tree. Well, dese chillun des lak all de rest. Dey hide in de bush, an' wait for hummin'-bird ter git 'mongst de fo'-o'clocks an' sech-like, an' dey run up an' try ter ketch 'em. Dey 'mos' ketch 'em, dey say, ev'y time; an' Marse William set up yon'er on de po'ch, an' look lak he los' his las' frien'. But dis here chile, de one in yon'er right now, she ain't lak nair 'nother chile ever come ter dis house. She was born ole, an' she do lak she please spite of ev'ybody. She was er-settin' up yon'er on top step wid er big lily in her han' yestiddy, an' done gone soun' ersleep, when 'long come ole Mis' Hummin'-bird an' smell her flower. She back off suspicious-like, but she come erg'in an' stick her head down in dere fer ter git de honey; an' 'bout dat time de chile wake up fum de hummin' of de wings,— mebbe she ain't been 'sleep,— an' clamp her han' down on dat flower, an' des scream one time an' ernother, loud as she could, lak she done gone plumb crazy : ' I got 'im! I got 'im! I got 'im, Uncle William! I

got 'im! I got 'im!' An' Marse William so skeered
he mos' fall over back'ards. 'Got what?' he say, 'got
what? Got er fit? Got er spasm?' An', Miss Helen,
she had 'im!

"Den Marse William come an' set down dere, feelin'
mighty bad. De hummin'-birds was his ma's special
pets forty years back, an' dey was his. Ain't nobody
ever hurt one on de place. He look solemn an' wor-
ried, 'cause his word was out. First thing he do was
ter onclench her fingers, an' he say: 'Soft, soft, my
chile, or you 'll kill 'im. Soft! Lemme see 'im; he
sha'n't git erway'— des so. An' he tear open de
flower an' give de bird some air. Den he sont me to
fetch de big glass kiver fum over de gole clock, an'
he put hit on de flo' wid de aidge prop up, an' ole Mis'
Hummin'-bird under hit. Lor'! but de chillun des
fell over one ernother lak somep'n' crazy, an' Marse
William had er job ter keep 'em fum breakin' de glass.
De little gyurl say den she mus' take de bird home
ter show her ma, an' Marse William look sad erg'in.
Bimeby he tell me ter watch de glass, an' he tell dat
chile ter wait: he mus' go roun' de corner an' inform
ole Mis' Hummin'-bird's chillun dat she been ketched,
an' dey need n' 'spec' ter see her no mo', an' not ter
wait supper for her. Little gyurl look mighty bad
when she hear dat; but bimeby she brighten up
an' say: 'I reck'n deir pa can take care of 'em.' An'
Marse William drop his eye on me an' shet his

lips tight; an' I knowed hit war n't no time ter laugh.

"But he go roun' de corner, tellin' all de chillun ter stay back, 'cause he promise ole Mis' Hummin'-bird long time ago not ter let nobody know where her house was hid."

"I 'm not sure," said Cæsar's listener, gravely, "that anything would justify a deception of that kind. I think that children should be told the truth."

"Lor'! Miss Helen, I 'spec' Marse William, if hit come ter er pinch, would tell er lie ter save er hummin'-bird, or his word. Anyhow, bimeby," continued Cæsar, laughing, "he come 'long back wid his han'k'-ch'ef up, an' say de hummin'-bird's chillun was carry-in' on so he could n' bear ter stay — said de baby of de fambly fairly moan an' sob lak hits po' little heart 'd break, an' she ask 'im ter please tell de little gyurl ter let her po' ma come 'long home an' nuss her, for she dat hongry she 'mos' perish for somep'n' ter eat. She say: 'Ask little gyurl how she lak for *her* little baby sister ter starve ter death, an' for somebody ter steal *her* ma while she off 'cross de street.' Well, missus, he 'mos' make *me* cry, hit soun' so natchul. An' de little gyurl sorter lif' de aidge of de glass higher an' higher while she was studyin' 'bout somep'n'— lif' hit des er little at er time, lak she can't he'p herse'f; an' ole Mis' Hummin'-bird bimeby see her way clear, an' gone lak er streak er grease' lightnin'. Well, ma'am,

de little gyurl fell ter cryin' den fit ter kill herse'f; but
Marse William ketch her up in his arms, an' tell her
he got somep'n' for her.   An' he go unlock de liberry,
an' take out fum er drawer er little silver whistle what
you put water in an' blow tell hit des fairly sings.
His ma gave him dat whistle when he was er little boy
hisse'f.   He take hit an' show her how hit work, an'
tell her how much better ter have somep'n' what can
sing lak all de birds, an' not er po' little hummin'-bird
what ain't good for nothin' 'cep'n' ter nuss her babies.
An' dat settles hit.   But de little gyurl done caught on
ter de blowin' herse'f, an' come 'long back dis mornin'.
She in yon'er now, blowin' fit ter kill — listen ! Hear
dat fuss ? An' he des as much destracted as if he
war n't dyin' ter sleep.   Yes, sah !" continued the old
man, lifting his voice as he heard his name called.
"I 'm er-comin'!   Des er-dyin' for sleep. Mornin',
missus ! Does me good ter see you sometimes. Lor' !
but you got yo' pa's walk — carry yo' head des lak
'im, high an' proud. Seem lak hit war n't but yestiddy
I seen Colonel Bailey stan'in' right dere in yo' tracks,
tellin' me, ' Cæsar, 'spec' some er dese days you goin'
ter have er new —' "

"Well, good-by, Cæsar; Mr. Marsdal is calling
again."

"Good-by, Miss Helen ! Yes, sah ! I 'm comin'!"

"Cæsar," said his master, gravely, when he did
come, "the young lady will honor us this morning

at breakfast. Put a suitable chair to the table for her." Seeing a troubled look upon the little face turned to his, he added: "And step across the street and say to her mother that I shall be greatly obliged if she will not interfere with the arrangement."

The child's face brightened, and the bird concert continued.

Out of the garret's dust came a child's high-backed chair to do duty for the tiny guest; out of the great china-closet, a little cup and saucer and plate, with their blue forget-me-nots and butterflies of gold; out of the velvet-lined recess behind the sliding panel in the wall where gleamed the old Marsdal silver, the little knife, fork, and spoon. For Cæsar's greatest value lay in. his quick perception of the fitness of things.

And such a breakfast as it was! There were the brownest of waffles, feathers in weight, cooled milk rich with cream, delicate broiled chicken, a golden omelet, and delicious rolls. Piled up about the vase of regal roses, behold the blended hues of the vineyard!

Long and wistfully the man watched his little guest and marked the workings of her mind. When Cæsar started the old ebony music-box, whose enfeebled spring failed in the middle of "What are the Wild Waves Saying?" she ceased for a while to eat, and resumed her whistle, to prove her loyalty; and when,

3

at last, as the wonderful hour was drawing to its
close, a humming-bird invaded the window, hovered
above a box of nasturtiums a moment, and, remembering perhaps the drama whispered of in bird circles
the day before, darted up a lane of sunlight to freedom
again, she looked grave and startled.

"Got to go now," she said suddenly; and sliding
from the chair, she trotted out into the hall, her little
feet making sweet music on the floor.

"Good-by!" he called to her. "Come again and
let the birds sing me asleep."

"Good-by!" floated back from her lips.

"What is it, Cæsar?" he asked of that worthy, who
was silently laughing.

"Gone ter see if anybody done ketched *her* ma."

"You have a mind, after all," said the gentleman,
turning quickly toward him. Then, "Go to the door
and see that she gets back across the street safely."

He was looking thoughtfully on the vacant chair;
perhaps he was dreaming some old dream anew, when
a vision dawned upon him. Clad in the softest,
whitest of muslins, with broad summer hat to match,
a rich glow upon her dark Southern face, balancing
on her hand a silver waiter full of blue celestial figs,
ripe and blushing peaches, and gorgeous pomegranates
laid open to their hearts, stood a young woman, the
daintier reproduction of Titian's daughter. Whether
she interrupted or completed his dream may not be

known. William Marsdal passed his hand across his eyes and came forward quickly. He took her face in both hands and kissed her forehead.

"Mother sends these with her best wishes," she said, "and as soon as convenient would like to see you."

"See me?" Then a smile came upon his lips. "I understand. Are you very happy, Marjory?"

But blushing Marjory, putting the waiter aside hurriedly, fled, looking back from the front door to kiss her hand.

FEW men have greater cause for congratulation than had William Marsdal at thirty. The only son in a family distinguished even in Southern society by its gentility and elegance, possessed of wealth and of a war record that would have made him a field-marshal under the Empire, he came home from years of study and travel, to take his father's place and face the responsibilities of life. Barring a slight haughtiness of manner which he wore in public, yet so perfectly blended with deferential courtesy that it did not offend, he was an ideal gentleman from even the critical standpoint of his own neighbors. It was understood that he would marry and settle down; and aside from the commotion in many a cote of shy doves, there was public interest in the fact that the old house would be again thrown open to society.

The old house had seen many a gay throng within its walls. Withdrawn behind the loveliness of its shrubbery it brooded now; but within doors were abundant evidences of refinement. The harmony of artistic natures was felt in the antique furnishings, and the total absence of the garish and bizarre; a good woman's heart, a good man's thought, spoke in all that hand or eye might rest upon, from ground to garret. Those whose tastes were not blunted by contact with the coarseness of life outside caught there the flavor of lives that had passed away. It takes many a year for a house to earn such a character — as long as it takes to make a gentleman. Dignity and that fine beauty which is called indefinable are axillary blossoms on family trees, and the home shares them. How soon, how easily, are they lost! A vulgar family can debauch such a house within a month, and break no civil law. Herein lies the gravest defect of the American system. There should be no way to sell the family home while the family lives; for within is the fountain-head of patriotism. That man who has a home full of memories and traditions is his country's sentinel.

To his home came William Marsdal, and people waited. Then, after some months, society said, "They were made for each other"— William and Helen, the only child of Colonel Marcus Bailey, whose little cottage was hidden behind the magnolias and roses a few hundred yards up the street, whose orchard of fine fruits broadened out in the rear until checked by the pasture for his splendid Jerseys, whose pasture was limited by spreading fields of cotton growing upon red levels, and whose cotton-fields — well, there is an end to all things, and the colonel's land ended somewhere.

Made for each other — that was the verdict. The verdict was seemingly indorsed; for soon the colonel was often seen taking his martial form, with assistance from his gold-headed cane, down to the Marsdals', and fanning himself upon the broad veranda, while old Mrs. Marsdal, with her lace cap above her aristocratic face, sat near, and they discussed the changes war had made, the solid South in Congress, and the alleged Ku-Klux. They discussed another matter with befitting dignity ; for Mrs. Marsdal mentioned her son's devotion to Helen, now apparent to everybody, and gave her host an impartial outline of William's character and a frank statement of his financial condition. The colonel said that William had always been a favorite of his, and that, however the young people might decide matters, he should be proud if Cupid brought about an alliance between his family and that of "Edward Marsdal,— God rest his soul,— than which no purer, broader, truer, ever animated the form of man." Whereupon Mrs. Marsdal gave him her hand a moment, and pressed a filmy kerchief to her eyes, in which tears rivaled the rays of the single diamond upon her thin finger. From this Cæsar felt authorized to launch upon the undercurrents of society the announcement of an engagement.

But the matter was not settled.

William and Helen were much together. He told

her of the scene upon the porch, and she blushed and
looked from him. He did not say the necessary word;
he did not know how. Any statement from him, he
felt, would be trite and useless. Could she not see
for herself? Was he not telling her his love every
day in the most eloquent of languages, the language
of the heart? Alas! he was fourteen years her senior,
and knew little of the girl's heart. He drifted with
the current, proud and happy. There were rivals,
and among them was Robert Delamar, a cotton factor
growing rich in the world of trade; and Robert was
confidently assiduous. But why should William fear
any of them? He had reason, but he did not know
it. Lacking the something in his make-up that ren-
ders self-analysis possible, Robert did not perceive
the truth of the situation. He had always been told
that he was handsome and irresistible; how could the
old planter's daughter fail to find him so? When,
one day, she gave him hesitatingly a conditional
yes, he was only surprised at the conditions and
at her refusal to add love's token.

The news came to William from a source he could
not doubt. Amazed, angry, sick at heart, he went to
Helen, and stood by her side a moment. She looked
away from him.

" Is it true?" he asked.

Her lips seemed not to move, but she whispered,
" Yes."

He was silent, the girl's bosom rising and falling with agitation. He lifted his hat, and went away. Her eyes sought him then, full of fright and anguish. She could not bring herself to speak. He never came again until fourteen years had passed, and, impoverished by speculation, broken-spirited, broken-hearted, Robert Delamar lay dying in the little cottage from excess of drink. Then he returned; for the dying man, with a clear perception of the truth and the nobility of his rival's heart, had sent for him. When he issued forth they were rivals no longer: one was dead, and the other a trustee and guardian.

The latter did his duty well. The fields had long before been sold; likewise the pasture and the orchard; and the cottage was mortgaged to its full value. How Robert Delamar had lived no one knew. But they came back — the orchard first, then the pasture, and then the red levels; and upon these levels, at William's command, the patient mules went to and fro as of old with the heavy plows, until the fields were white with the summer snows of the South. One day the mortgage fell away from the little cottage, and a thrill of delight ran through the town; for, with all their bickerings, jealousies, and heartburnings, the people in these old towns love one another and the past.

But William Marsdal was another man in most respects. From the blow delivered by a woman's hand he shrank back and back within himself and the old home, until he almost disappeared from public view. The mantle of haughtiness became as mask and mail of iron. Still, as a rule, coldly polite, he developed an irritability that made politeness difficult; and there were times when, impatient from interference or the neighborly efforts of uncongenial persons to be friendly, he lost restraint. As the years passed he found it easier to be alone. People accepted him as an eccentric, explosive man with whom it was unsafe to trifle, but upon whom every one might rely to do the right thing at last in the wrong way.

And yet they loved him! Little Marjory Delamar, his ward, soon learned to brave the dragon for the wonders of the Marsdal house. He was no dragon with her. She called him "Uncle William"; and as, one by one, she led in her playmates, they called him "Uncle William" too, and none were afraid; for, tolerating the boys, he became at last almost the slave of the little girls. People outside, who had felt the man's irascibility, his biting sarcasm, and the thunders of his resentment, laughed to see his softer side. They came to realize that, like some strong tree crowded by wall or cliff, he was developing toward all the sunshine that could reach him. In these years no child's demand ever went unnoticed by William Marsdal. Can any one ever forget the time when, losing a day by an accident, John Robinson's circus

thought to slight the old town for a rival in red and
yellow paint, twenty miles away—and this after the
bills were up, and William Marsdal's promise had
lain for weeks next to the hearts of the children who
wore his flowers? Not one of them, at least. They
were frightened and distressed, it is true, by the bad
news and William's strange disappearance, and they
paid many an anxious visit to Cæsar, much to that
worthy's discomfiture. One day there was a blare of
trumpets, and William Marsdal rode into town upon
his big black horse at the head of the circus procession, pointed out a site for the tent in his own pasture, went around and adjourned the schools, closed
up business houses, and gave a free performance.
The glory of that day was William's, for had he not
vanquished an impudent rival, and plucked victory
from defeat? But with William the glorious feature
of the day was the bank of young girls rising to the
canvas roof itself, their faces radiant with delight,
their ribbons and tresses dancing under the swaying
cloth, their little hands beating time to the music of
the scarlet band.

He was the king! For at his command the lady in
short skirts came back twice on the clay-bank horse
and waltzed through rings of living flame; the trained
dogs went through their antics over and over; and
the trick-mule stayed in the ring until too tired to
kick. He cornered for his small guests the market

for peanuts and lemonade; and as though this were not enough, he gave Cæsar to the clown to make more fun for them. But when the clown climbed the ropes for his present, and Cæsar, half afraid, resisted, and they rolled together in the dust, and the smallest girls began to cry, he bought Cæsar back for five dollars — extortion, he called it — and stilled the rising tumult. Oh, the rapture of that day!

There was the recent affair of the new church organ. How violently, sarcastically, almost venomously, he opposed the purchase! And yet, when the committee lacked sixty per cent. of the needed amount, and the local sheet outlined a church fair, he called in Marjory, one day, and sent her with a check for the sixty per cent., and a message to the effect that as between two evils he chose the lesser one.

Marjory was twelve when she became the ward of this strange man. Now she was eighteen; and as, rigidly erect in his faultless dress, he walked to the cottage responsive to her mother's summons, a long procession of events filed past him in review. But he could count upon the fingers of one hand the times he had been to the cottage since Helen's marriage: when Robert Delamar died; when he was buried; when the trust began; and, finally, when, freed from all encumbrances and productive, the little property was turned over to its former owner. This was the fifth time; he would make it the last.

And Robert Delamar had been six years dead!

He lifted the latch and passed along the gravel walk to the house, and then into the living-room. The woman who entered was Helen Bailey grown older. He held her hand a moment, while her eyes rested upon him with a sad, inquiring gaze that he seemed to understand. It was a gaze that, passing rapidly over his attire, touched for a moment the thin gray hair upon his temples, and rested upon the stern, uncompromising lines of his face. He could not endure even the suggestion of pity in her. He flushed for an instant, and the perpendicular line between his eyes deepened; but the gentility of his race quickly swept away all resentment.

"I thank you, Helen," he said, "for your kind remembrance this morning, and dear Marjory's bright face. How can I serve you?"

Her sad smile came back; for a woman at thirty-eight is wiser than most men at fifty-two. She hesitated.

"Cæsar tells me you are not well. Is it serious?"

"Cæsar is a babbling fool, Helen! I have suffered a little from insomnia for the week past."

"You have not slept at all! But be seated. There must be some cause for this," she continued. "You should consult a physician, Mr. Marsdal. Let me insist that you see a physician."

A grim smile came upon his face. "And you have one that you can recommend, I suppose."

"Oh," she laughed, "yes. But I had forgotten. It is of him I wish to speak. He told me," she said, looking down, "that you had given your consent to his marriage with Marjory; and now I have to tell you — that — circumstances — render it almost necessary for the marriage to take place soon. In fact, they have selected the date two weeks from to-day. Henry is going North and abroad for several years' study and hospital practice, and —"

"I see. Let them go."

He said this so bluntly that the woman resented it with flashing eyes.

"That is your reply?" she asked, somewhat coldly. "I thought you would be more interested, at least."

"I am sufficiently interested. I have neglected nothing. I know who Henry Vernon is, and his family for four generations back. I knew them when he came to me; for I am not blind, and found out in advance. And when I gave my consent, he signed a contract that will, in a measure, protect her. There is no longer any need of delay. He is able and keen in his profession; that is, he is an accomplished humbug. But I make no complaint. He is a necessary evil."

"I see you are still unchanged in your opinion of physicians."

"Entirely so. Will you be pleased to read the contract? I guessed at the nature of your business, and brought it with me."

"I shall be glad to read it," she said, surprised.

He drew forth a document and handed it to her. It was in his own well-known handwriting, she saw. She read:

In consideration of William Marsdal's consent to my marriage to his ward, Marjory Delamar, before she is of age, I hereby agree that one week after said marriage I will send her back to her mother to remain twenty-four hours. If upon the expiration of that time she fails to return to me, I pledge my honor as a gentleman never again to seek her presence or attempt to communicate with her, and that I will consent to a legal separation without prejudice. If she does return to me, then at the expiration of two years she shall again return to her mother for one day, upon the same terms. And I hereby give to this contract all legal force possible, making it a part of the religious contract yet to be solemnized, and will faithfully abide by it.

[Signed]   HENRY VERNON.

Helen looked up from the paper, startled and embarrassed.

"How strange!" she whispered. "And yet—"

"I told him," continued William Marsdal, "that the average marriage credited to a heavenly making was a slander upon God Almighty; that a woman at eighteen knows nothing, and my object was to save something of life for my child if she erred in her judgment. The fellow agreed with me instantly,"— he paused and stared at his listener, as though not yet recovered from astonishment,— "and I had never

liked him until then. He said he would sign anything that would throw safeguards about Marjory's
future; that the husband was the only danger from
which the law did not guard a woman. A man with
a heart and mind like that ought to abandon hum-
buggery."

"It was thoughtful of you — thoughtful of you,"
said Helen.

"The idea did not originate with me. I only carried out the unformed plan of your husband, revealed
in his last moments."

She made no reply to this. Her breath came in
gasps for one instant, and then she buried her face in
her handkerchief and wept silently.

He came to her side. "Yes, Helen; Robert Delamar saw his mistake when life's perspective was complete. All that he could do was to turn it to account
for his daughter's sake. You were a good wife, a
devoted wife, to him. Look up! I have told you the
truth to — hallow his memory." After a few moments' silence, he continued: "I have two requests,
Helen, to make of you : I want Marjory to wear this,"
— he held out an exquisite little coronet set with diamonds,—"and I wish her marriage to take place in
my house. It is eminently proper that it should,
since I am her guardian, and your house is small. I
want to see her a bride, crowned with these jewels, in
the home of William Marsdal. I bought the trinket

more than twenty years ago. You will not refuse me!" He wavered slightly, and pressed his hand to his brow, a look of confusion in his eyes; but before she could reach him with outstretched hand he had steadied himself.

"Won't you let Henry come to see you, Mr. Marsdal? You are really ill. Don't refuse *me*. I refuse you nothing."

He felt in his pocket and handed her some papers.

"Here," said he, "are expressed a week's efforts to calculate a year's interest upon a simple note for six hundred and ninety dollars. The interest gets bigger and bigger every time, and upon the first trial it was greater than the principal. Something slipped in here," he said, touching his forehead, "and since then I have n't slept. If Henry can prescribe for bad arithmetic, send him around."

At the door he turned, to find her, sad and distressed, watching him. "Let nothing delay the marriage," he said.

III

KEEN, quick, modern, well balanced, and bold, a healer by intuition and a physician by conscientious acquisition, Henry Vernon had begun his professional life with the conviction that failure was impossible. He grasped the new solutions of old problems, and placed himself in harmony with the new methods as fast as he could master them; and he mastered everything he attempted until he met with William Marsdal. Behind the abruptness, the cynicism, and the sarcasm of this man he found an intellectual force and perception unsuspected, an ego unknown, unknowable, and elusive. Moreover, he found a disbeliever in the claims made for medicine. This opposing combination of forces placed him at great disadvantage when he came to study into the disorder which affected the sick man. There was another disadvantage: he had not been called; he had been sent. The pressure was behind. On the other hand, he and William Marsdal were practically of one family, and that fact, with the ironical message accompanying the arithmetical attempts, must perforce suffice for excuse to beard the lion in his den; and putting aside pride, he bearded him.

4

William Marsdal grasped the young man's situation at once, and something like a smile hovered about his mouth when he contemplated the swarthy, square-jawed professional. How the data for a diagnosis were obtained Dr. Vernon could never entirely recall; but a dozen times during the hour he was sorely tempted to pick up his hat and leave without ceremony. Yet his host's outward manner was perfect. Still, he seemed to be fencing with an unfriendly antagonist in the dark, and despite a determination and promise to keep his temper, he from time to time received thrusts and blows that were maddening. Only the memory of Marjory and the undoubted goodness of the older man sustained him. But he satisfied himself at last that his first suspicions were correct. Armed with his conviction, he was on better ground. He suited his action to the strong character before him.

"Mr. Marsdal," he began, "I have to tell you that you are not only ill, but threatened with a serious danger. It is best to tell you so frankly."

"Right so far, my young friend. Proceed."

"It may be paresis. It may be a growing tumor. It may be the effects of a slight lesion that will pass away by absorption, or a trifling inflammation that ten hours' sleep will relieve. Whatever it is, it is in the brain."

William Marsdal laughed. "It is but another way

of saying that I consider you a very able man, sir, when I say again I agree with you. Proceed."

"My advice is to board the first train with a competent nurse, and go to a specialist in New York under whom I studied. If any one can cure you, he is the man."

"I won't go. What next?"

"Then you must put your life in my hands."

"Ah! That 's another question. What do you propose to do with it, young man?"

"Preserve it."

"I see — I see. Modest, but still it is to the point. However, I won't do that, either."

This was one of the times that Dr. Vernon reached for his hat, but he changed his mind. He looked his unwilling patient straight in the eyes.

"You said yes to me, Mr. Marsdal, when I asked you for Marjory Delamar, and at the same time told me she was dearer to you than life itself. I believe those were the words? But you seem to be more careful of your life than of your ward, after all."

The slightly raised eyebrows and distinct sarcasm, the impudence of it all, astonished his hearer so that for a moment he could but stare. William Marsdal had one profane word that he used on extra occasions, and on this occasion he used it eloquently.

"I would not swear," said the young man, coolly, "unless for amusement. Avoid every form of mental excitement. There is too much excitement now, or you would sleep. My remark was not irrelevant nor intended for impertinence. I said you must put your life in my hands, but I did not say that I would accept the trust. I would do it only upon conditions. These might not suit you. There are other doctors in town—"

"All humbugs!"

"As you please. I have nothing else to suggest. I sincerely desire to help you for reasons you know in advance, but I cannot do it by main force."

"Young man," said William Marsdal, after a moment of silence, during which he perhaps tried to get his own consent to apologize for the profanity, "you may have diagnosed my present malady correctly, but there are other things in there besides tumors and lesions and inflammation. There is a love for Marjory Delamar that escaped you. If William Marsdal puts his life in your hands, and you lose it, your future, in this town, is ruined. You would never survive the tongues of your professional brethren. My interest in the matter lies in the fact that professional ruin for you would cast a shadow over Marjory's future. My life is of little value; it shall not become a menace to her. I know my case; it is serious. Nothing but sleep can save me." His manner had changed. For one moment he was grave and serious.

Touched to the heart, amazed, repentant, Dr. Vernon sat silent, looking upon the floor.

"Think no more of it," said the host. "Come in
occasionally with Marjory, and suggest — mind you,
I say suggest — things to try. If I get well, I'll tell
the world you saved me. If I die, you can tell them
that it happened because I would n't let you." His
old manner had returned.

So the matter arranged itself. But sleep would not
come to the tired brain. All medical remedies failed.
And the days passed.

The singular illness of William Marsdal soon became the absorbing topic of the town. He was
amazed to find how many friends he had, and was
touched by their loving solicitude; and then he raved
to Cæsar about the annoyance. Every one was for-
bidden the yard but Marjory and her fiancé, and the
children. The little ones tiptoed in and gathered
flowers as usual. They even invaded the cool sitting-
room, and looked into the haggard face for the old
smile, and found it. A thousand remedies were suggested, and one day the little girl across the street broke
loose from restraining hands and brought another.
She sat upon the carriage-step and gravely took off
her shoes, and then went in, slamming the gate with
a little extra force — so it seemed to Cæsar. She passed
noiselessly on till she found her friend stretched upon
the leather lounge, waiting. She had remembered his
remark about the birds.

"Going to let the birds sing you to sleep," she said
positively.

He turned his head quickly, not having heard her enter the room, and he laughed silently.

"Good! I have tried everything else!" he said. "Now, I 'll shut my eyes tight, and you make the birds sing; and when I get to sleep, you can slip out and go home and tell them you beat the town. I 'm ready; go ahead." And with a smile still upon his face, he shut his eyes.

The little girl made the birds sing. Cæsar felt that their shrill voices would never, never cease. But the invalid, judging from his facial expression, was floating in a sea of bliss. At last, however, her breath gave out. Coming close to her friend, she said: "Are you asleep?"

"Sound asleep," he replied. "Tell the birds I 'm *so* much obliged."

Full of the glory of her conquest, the child ran off. Cæsar watched her out of the gate.

"Oomhoo!" he said. "Done lef' dem shoes settin' out dere."

That meant a trip across the street for Cæsar.

Dr. Vernon came up that evening with Marjory, bringing a message from her mother, and a waiter of fruit. The next day was the marriage-day. Their plans had been changed; for William Marsdal would not listen to a postponement, and the doctor would not consider the performance of the ceremony in that house under the circumstances. The old Presbyterian church had been substituted.

"Since I have been lying here," the sick man said, maintaining his playfulness, "I have been wondering how I could have ever been so sleepy that I could n't hold up my head; and yet I remember distinctly that, as a boy, there were times when I thought I should die if they did n't *let* me sleep. My parents were strict church-people, and I being an only child, they tried all sorts of experiments with me." He laughed silently over some memory, and continued: "Sunday was to me a nightmare. I had to be scrubbed by the nurse before breakfast, have my ears bored out with a finger concealed in a coarse towel, and study my Sunday-school lesson. At nine o'clock I was taken down to the school,— same old school going on now every Sunday under the same old church up the street,— and very much as Abraham took Isaac into the mountains to be sacrificed. At ten they led me up-stairs for the two hours of prayer and sermon. How sleepy I used to get!— for I was only a little fellow at that time. My feet could n't touch the floor of the pew, and my back would n't reach the pew's back. I knew about as much of what was going on as a cow does of astronomy. I would sit up, and wave to the right and left, and bob forward, and my father or mother would straighten me up patiently and frown. There was a Greek border around the ceiling — I saw the same thing in Italy when first I went abroad, and it made me homesick — that I played was a boulevard, and I drove my pony around the church, nearly twisting my head off when he went behind the organ, and twisting it back in a complete circle to see him come out on the other side. And there was a circle in the center of the ceiling where I raced him. Sometimes he went so fast I would get dizzy and fall against mother, to be firmly elbowed up again, and reproved with a grave face and compressed lips. Sometimes I would look at the cushioned seat and think that if I could just stretch out at full length there, with my head in mother's lap, I should be willing to die for it. But I was too much frightened to try it, for in front of me was a being of great power. He was bald on the top of his head, with his hair roached forward over his temples, and wore a high stock that kept him from turning his head. The sunlight would come down through the round panes of colored glass above the tall windows and crown him with changing glories; and it is a fact that I picked him out as the person intended when the preacher spoke of an awful being whose face was forever hid from the eyes of man. When prayer-time came, I prayed to him from behind. I do not remember that I ever learned his name."

So the excited brain worked and worked, throwing off old impressions as one who digs in the garden up-turns roots and bulbs, mementos of a bygone spring. Dr. Vernon listened intently, his brow in his hand,

his face in the shadow. To him the pictured scenes
were themselves symptoms. He could have placed
his finger upon the localities of the brain that were
affected. As, with Marjory, he walked home under
the stars, he was strangely silent and thoughtful for
one so near the realization of his dream. Marjory
wondered and was piqued. It was the first but not
the last time that a jealous mistress interfered with
her plans.

"Will you give me an hour to-morrow?" he asked.
"I am going to try an experiment."

"Certainly, Henry; but to-morrow will be my
busiest day."

"I know, but my experiment is for William Marsdal. You noticed that the progress of his malady
has reached the mysterious records of youth; the
little cells are giving back their impressions. I want
to try and uncover some that will exert a good influence. I will explain to-morrow."

"Just to oblige me, Uncle William. It is not far,
and the walk will do you good. You have not heard
the new organ, and you have never heard Marjory
play. Don't refuse; remember that this is the last
day your little girl —"

"Get my hat."

Marjory danced off delighted, and the two set out,
William Marsdal still erect, but thin and haggard,

and the old defiant look in his eyes changed to that
of a hunted animal. Still his splendid strength sustained him.

But few passers-by saw the two, and those who did
supposed they were strolling for exercise only. They
went into the old church, and Dr. Vernon joined them
by what was apparently a mere chance.

"Have you memory enough," he said, smiling, "to
find your boyhood's scene of suffering?"

William Marsdal had been standing, gazing about
him abstractedly, thinking of the long-gone days.

"Yes," he said gravely, and together they walked
to the pew he designated. Again he sat in the familiar
spot. "It is more comfortable now. I can touch
the floor and the back both. Nothing else appears
changed. Dear me! dear me! but where are the
faces, the forms, I knew? Forty years! It is a long
time, and yet it was but yesterday!"

"I must not tire you," said Marjory, obeying a
signal from Dr. Vernon. "I'll run up and try the
organ now."

As she began to play, William Marsdal looked back
and upward to where he could see her curls above
the rail.

Marjory made the beautiful instrument sing all the
old-time tunes. Dr. Vernon excused himself to "keep
an engagement," but he stood outside in the vestibule,
and through a half-opened door watched the little

scene within. And this is what he saw: The sick man sat dreaming in the pew, his chin in his hand, for many minutes. and then he began idly to study the surroundings, having forgotten the music and the player. His face was lifted, and his eyes followed in its zigzag course the Greek border under the ceiling — the boulevard of his boyhood days. Then they appeared to find the big circle. A half-smile lit his face; his clinical aspect improved. He lowered his head and sank into reverie, and time and again he lifted it and went through the familiar pantomime. But when many minutes had passed, and the fair player was gently drawing from the instrument the strains of that sadly beautiful old hymn, "Come, ye disconsolate," Dr. Vernon started forward quickly: the figure in the pew had distinctly swayed. Instantly it recovered and was rigid. And then again the unmistakable motion made in nodding was apparent. William Marsdal was decidedly sleepy. He appeared to struggle with his weakness; then he involuntarily yielded. He did that which brought a smile of delight to the young man's face: he looked about him cautiously, measured the cushion with his eye, and, with sudden surrender of his scruples, calmly stretched himself out at full length. Dr. Vernon rushed noiselessly, breathlessly, to the organ-loft.

"Play on! play on!" he whispered eagerly, for Marjory's pretty mouth and eyes were open, and she was pausing in sheer astonishment. But she rallied, and played "Come, ye disconsolate," over and over and over, until she almost dropped from the seat. Then Henry came up again, radiant and joyful.

"Thank God, he sleeps!" he said. "Don't stop! don't stop yet!"

She made only one false note, which was doing well when kisses were being showered upon her lips and her head was drawn back.

"Keep a thread of music running through his dream, dear; one hand will do — chords, fifths. I am afraid of silence. Oh, if I could pray, I believe I should try the Presbyterians' long prayer!"

She had never seen him in this mood. "Henry!" she said reprovingly.

And then he uttered an exclamation that was not a prayer, and dashed down-stairs again; for a dozen girls, laden with flowers, had passed into the church, and were preparing to decorate for Marjory's marriage. In a moment he was among them, and they were silenced with six words: "William Marsdal is asleep at last!" But he suffered them to pass noiselessly through the aisles, and wreathe altar, lamp-stands, and brackets with flowers, and fill the vases.

It was a strange scene for that dim old church: the girls in white, working so swiftly, silently, intelligently, banishing the sadness of the solitude with their regal blossoms. It was as though Spring with her handmaidens had come into the little world. When all was ended, and the physician stood over the sleeper with lifted hand, the fairies glided by, each with a tender look into the familiar face touched with the violet hues of the painted glass, and were gone. In their stead were the odor of flowers, the gleam of white blossoms, and the thread of melody descending from above.

So slept the sick man; and another problem arose. The bride was forced away, and, later, friends took the place of the groom. A guard stood at the door to bar intruders and answer questions, and one in the street to bar all vehicles. Noon's short shadows lengthened toward the east, and the sun set. As the hour for the ceremony drew near, the physician ruled the groom. Henry Vernon declared that no consideration would tempt any of those interested to awaken the sleeper: that was out of the question. "Postpone the wedding? No," said he, promptly, "that will excite him when he does awake. We will carry out his original plan."

So they went to work again. This time Cæsar slaved for the fairies. The old Marsdal mansion was thrown open, and the windows flashed outward their lights for the first time in many a year. A young bride wearing a tiara of diamonds stood beneath the smilax, an old man's dream made visible, and was married to the man she loved. Nine o'clock rang as she gave him her pledge, and she did not notice a slight commotion near the door. But when the prayer was ended, and, pushing back her veil, she faced the phalanx of well-wishing friends, she saw standing there William Marsdal, his face bright with the dews of rest, his eyes lit by the old familiar flame. With a cry she ran to him and hid her head upon his breast, sobbing with happiness. He could but kiss her forehead over and over, and whisper. He turned from the eager congratulations pouring in upon him, and from the forms about him.

"Kind friends," he said, "you caught William Marsdal napping. I missed some sleep forty years ago, but I caught up to-day. Enjoy yourselves; the house is yours." He retired precipitately, and hid himself in the shadow of the Lamarque at the far end of the veranda to recover his equanimity. As he stood there he felt a touch upon his arm, and, looking down, saw in a little patch of moonlight the face of Helen Bailey.

"I am so glad," she said, "I must tell you! And, Mr. Marsdal, we have not met often; we may not meet again. I want to thank you—oh, I wish I could thank you for your kindness to me and my child! I did not deserve it—I did not, I did not!" She covered her face with her hands, and stood in the shadow.

"Helen," he said, "how could you do it?" The

question crying for utterance so long had burst from him at last.

"Oh," she said brokenly, "you did not understand — no man understands! I wanted to be asked, to be wooed — every girl wishes that. It was all so matter-of-fact — and I was proud! If you had spoken one word — that day — oh, if you had touched me with your hand, I would have thrown myself into your arms!"

"What!" he cried. "You loved me?"

"Every minute of my life since I met you!"

"And I," he said, in awe, as the sad mistake began to be apparent, "thought that my fourteen years — that I was too old. I thought that the trouble was there!"

She did not speak, but stood struggling with her emotion. He came and put his hand reverently upon her head.

"Helen," he said, "in the hours of that blessed sleep in the old church I dreamed of you. My mind ran all the way up from childhood to those happy days of ours; and I thought I saw you standing in this house a bride. I got no further than that. I awoke with the moon looking down into my face, and came away happy and yet sad. Is it too late for that dream to come true? Let me see your face."

And he saw it with the love-light shining through wet lashes.

"To-night," he whispered — "let it be to-night!"

She was too much amazed to answer.

Then William Marsdal was himself again. "It shall be to-night, now, madam! You have robbed me of twenty years. You shall not rob me of another day."

Her protestations were useless. She found herself laughing and half indignant over her situation; but resistance was useless. He marched her in through a side-window, and stood by while she laved her eyes and arranged her hair, and he checked her frequent rebellions in their incipiency. When he took her into the broad parlor, and, standing where the young couple had just stood, announced his intention, there was almost a cheer from the assemblage; for the romance in his life was a town legend. And under the smilax, in a silence that was almost too solemn, William Marsdal's dream came true.

Little more remains to be told. Society was shaken to its foundation, of course; and then it smiled over the affair, which it called thoroughly Marsdalesque; for who else could have looked death in the face at 9 A. M., and a bride at 9 P. M., and in the meantime have secured twelve hours of sleep?

Cæsar came out on the sidewalk next morning to sweep the carriage-step, and found a good-looking mulatto woman similarly engaged across the street.

"Tell de little gyurl Marse William done ketch er hummin'-bird hisse'f up on de same po'ch," he said. "Ketched her once befo', an' turn her loose. Bet he don't turn her loose no more!"

"Cæsar!" called an imperative voice from the porch.

"Yes, sah!"

"Carry these roses down to your Miss Helen, with my compliments, and say that I will call for her with the carriage at ten o'clock!"

ISAM AND THE MAJOR

READERS of this story may possibly recall an introduction, several years ago, to Major Crawford Worthington and his vade-mecum Isam, in a story entitled "Two Runaways," wherein was related how the eccentric bachelor cotton-planter was induced to run away, one summer, with his sly old negro; how they lived the somewhat lawless life of marooners in the swamp, reveling in fish-chowders, green corn, poultry, melons, and fruits, to say nothing of mint-juleps and corn-cob pipes; how they fought the deer, and their providential rescue; and how for the time being their social relations were suspended and they were boys again, "loose and free." Many sympathetic people tied down to the desks and the sedentary occupations of the city, who annually feel the impulse to savagery beat afar off among the mysteries of inherited memories, and many interested in the plantation life of ante-bellum times, have expressed a desire to hear something more of the lives of these worthies.

Now, ordinarily, the mere expression of such a desire, however unanimously, would not justify an intrusion upon the home life and privacies of any one, certainly not upon those of a man like Major Crawford Worthington; and the writer, under this conviction, has steadily refused, during several years, to violate further the sanctity of Woodhaven; but recently his scruples have been removed by very ingenious arguments. It is said that the major belongs to history, that he is part of the times, that no one else now will write his history, for fear of trespassing on the work that has already been done, and that the public is as much entitled to all of him as it is to a part. The same arguments apply with equal force to Isam. But the most potent argument is that the public has rather underestimated the character of the master of Woodhaven while laughing at his foibles, and that a complete picture is now due him.

These conclusions have induced the writer to undertake, with much careful labor, to secure subsequent facts in the lives of Major Crawford Worthington and Isam, and to place them on record. The first chapters describe a great change in the personnel at Woodhaven, and probably the most momentous fact in its daily history for many a long year.

I

MAJOR WORTHINGTON sat upon his broad back porch, some three months after his runaway with Isam, his fat left leg across the seat of a second chair that he had drawn into service, his left arm resting upon its back. This was his favorite posture, and when he assumed it he was prepared to receive, if not always with composure, still without trepidation, the developments of the day in their regular order. To-day he ought to have been moderately content and serene, for there was in reflection and about him much suggestive of peace and quiet. The year had been a prosperous one for planters. The cotton had done well; the great corn-fields, stripped of their fodder, waited only the last round of the wagons to yield up the ripened grain; no unusual amount of sickness had fallen upon his three hundred negroes; and the Whigs had scored an important point on the Democrats. But it was easy to see that all these blessings had not sufficed to shut out disturbing thoughts from the mind of the gentleman, nor was the direct source of the disturbance concealed. A letter lay in his free hand, and he was intently studying the Texas postmark, which, could

frowns have effected it, would have been quickly
obliterated. But frowns cannot change inanimate
forms, and so the Texas postmark continued to look
the major full in the face with composure, while setting in motion a train of disturbing thoughts. In
some mysterious way it connected itself with the pre-
vious evening, when, sitting as he was at that moment, an incident occurred, the details of which rose
in mind with singular vividness.

A pile of pine-knots had blazed beneath him in the
broad back yard, and the negroes danced under his
laughing eye for the prize he had offered. While
the scene was still animated with leaping forms, and
vocal with songs and shouts, out of the shadow into
the red glare of the firelight had come an old ne-
gress, tall and straight indeed, but tremulous with
the weight of nearly a century, and faced him at the
foot of the steps. With her presence came a sudden
silence, for she possessed an influence over the rude
people assembled there, rooted in fear and trust.
Living alone on a distant part of the plantation, yet,
as may be readily understood, in absolute security,
she healed and cured the sick with her secret herbs,
and warded off invisible evils with the magic of potent charms; for the faith cure is older than civiliza-
tion. Filling an important position in the economy
of the place, an inheritance herself, she possessed, by
custom, rights that even the master recognized as

vested, and a liberty as complete as his own. The significance of her appearance in the yard lay in the extreme rarity of its occurrence, and in the superstition common among the slaves that it foretold always an important change for good or evil in the family. That Major Worthington credited this common belief cannot be affirmed. He was aware of the fact that coincidences in the past somewhat justified it, but the question lay among those undebated ones that every mind carries indifferently. He would have hooted at such a belief, and if charged with it by any one, the rash person would undoubtedly have heard himself denounced as a fool of the species *condemnatus*. Yet family traditions never altogether fade from the memory of any member, and they exert, to some degree, an influence upon the mind, unconscious though it be. So it was that as the dancers paused, and the dim and murky eyes of the old woman were turned upon him, he said kindly:

"Come in, Aunt Silvy; I 'm glad to see you."

She stood silent, turning her head about slowly upon the crowd, face after face averting itself uneasily as it met her gaze, her failing mind gradually connecting the incidents necessary to comprehension. Seeing that the sport was spoiled by her presence, the major ordered Isam to bring some sugar, coffee, tobacco, and whisky for the old creature. Taking them from the steps where Isam had placed them,

Aunt Silvy.

and from which he had precipitately retired, she began to retrace the way toward her lonely cabin; but remembering her art, she turned slowly and looked back, nodding her head.

"Let the win' pass," she said grandly, and with startling energy. "When hit is gone —" The rest of the sentence sank into an unintelligible mumble.

It was impossible to lift the spell of her visit from the superstitious spirits about him, and so, after one or two vain attempts, Major Worthington dismissed them with an explosion of several of his expressive anathemas, and relighted his pipe. For an hour he sat and smoked, smiling occasionally when he remembered Isam's hurried retreat up the steps. But he noticed, from time to time, that the wind blew steadily, and his mind drifted back into other days. Once in the night he awoke; the wind was still blowing.

To-day, as he sat holding the unopened letter, these events came back to memory with a persistence that annoyed him. Before breaking the seal he cast a glance about him. The yellowed leaves of the china-tree, yielding to the still active breeze, swarmed outward and downward into the cotton, which, beginning just outside the yard fence, stretched away in nodding ranks to the distant woodland. Where the negro pickers bent over the white staple, a bright turban here and there gave back flashes of color, and the regular cadence of their song rose and fell as the breeze freshened or died away under the melodious sounds. The single sweet-gum tree in the fence corner, its high lifted crest and widely extended branches bending and dipping slowly in the haze of the fading day, was crimson, scarlet, and yellow. Under it, upon the top rail, a red-and-yellow rooster, in pleasing harmony with his surroundings, was resisting the pressure of the wind upon his broad tail, and calling to his family to follow him into the shadowy branches above. On the very top of the gin-house beyond, his brush spread against the darkened roof, stood the stately pea-fowl, and ever and anon his unequaled plumage, lifted as by an unseen hand, received the slanting sunbeams, and made a glory against the sky.

The man was not given to the study of these things. His eye embraced rather than sought out the details of the picture as he lifted it from the letter responsive to a sudden thought. There was motion everywhere, for the wind still blew; and drawing forth his penknife, he inserted it in the corner of the envelop. Just at that moment, as though no longer meeting a resisting pressure in the air, the refrain of the picker floated in, clear and distinct:

> Ring dem sweet shinin' bells,
> Ring dem sweet bells!

and a single petal from the Lamarque rose-bush at the end of the porch, planted many years ago by a little sister, forsaken in mid-air by its fickle lover, fluttered down and lay upon his hand. Looking up quickly, he saw that absolute stillness lay upon every object. The wind had passed. He drew his knife-blade along the envelop, and read the inclosure.

As Isam came and went noiselessly across the porch, his wrinkled face and grizzly beard were often turned toward his master without attracting attention. Something in the calm, unbroken mood there revealed began to impress him as remarkable. His comings, from one excuse or another, grew more frequent, and presently an anxious look began to creep into his own face. Finally he ceased to go, and stood watching his master, more and more puzzled. He drew nearer, and his soft, insinuating voice broke the silence.

"Mas' Craffud?"

There was no reply.

"Mas' Craffud, is yer sick, honey?"

Still no reply.

The old negro's eye caught a glimpse of the letter that had slipped to the floor. He took it up and examined it critically. It was plain to his mind that the key to this new, strange mood lay in the lines of that sheet. He withdrew softly to the dining-room, and put on his silver-rimmed spectacles for a better examination. An hour before he had brought the semi-weekly mail from Milledgeville, and evidently this

was one of the letters. But Isam's education was not
equal to the unraveling of the mystery hidden in the
few words there recorded. He went quickly through
the hall, and found old Hebe in the sewing-room, busy
with the rough garments of the slaves, the unending
labor of a lifetime, now grown to be necessary to her
happiness.

"What dat paper say, mammy ? " he asked anxiously, thrusting the message into her hand, and
seating himself beside her. The old woman looked
at him indignantly.

"Git off dem clothes, boy! Ain't yer got no better
manners den ter come drop down on folks's things
like dat ? "

Her great age gave her authority, and even Isam
was a boy in her memory.

"Hit 's done come! hit 's done come!" he cried,
excitedly drawing the garments from beneath him
and throwing them aside. A presentiment was
strengthening in his keen mind. "Read hit, mammy!
read hit ! "

She looked at him over her glasses in wonder.

"What business you got readin' young marster's
letters, you black rascal ? "

"'T ain't no time to talk, mammy," he said earnestly, his features working nervously; "Mas' Craffud down in de low grounds out yonder, all tore
up 'bout dat letter." He looked around cautiously,

" It was Isam's way of meeting grief."

and lowered his voice. "Aunt Silvy hyah las'
night —"

He paused to watch Hebe's face. She began to
read, exercising an accomplishment that dated back to
childhood and the kindness of a long-dead mistress.
Her progress was slow, for her practice had been
confined chiefly to the open print of her Bible; but
she gathered the sense of the message surely, for, as
she contemplated it in silence, her face grew agitated
and her hand began to tremble. Then, clutching the
letter tightly, and moaning, she stood up.

"Who dead?" Isam grasped her arm.

At the sound of the word she broke into a wail
that rang through the house.

"Dead! dead! dead! She won't come back no
more now! She won't come back no more!"

The old man understood. He threw both hands to
his head, and rushed from the house. Straight he
went across the yard, behind the smoke-house, and
crouched upon the wash-bench there. It was Isam's
way of meeting grief.

But Hebe went upon the porch, her wail growing
louder as her excitement increased. She approached
the silent figure, and placed her hand upon his
shoulder. The cook and several of the washerwomen
came to the foot of the steps, and added their voices
to hers, clapping hands and bending bodies in rhyth-
mical unison. But the tumult did not change the

mood of the silent man. He had heard it too often sounded about those steps, or out in the quarters, when, one by one, members of the family lay dead in the darkened parlors.

"All gone now! all gone but one!"

It was Hebe's voice. Something in the words drew his attention for the first time, and his eyes sought her face. Animated by a memory, with the recollection of an enforced silence extending through long years, and a never-dying love tugging at her heart-strings, she turned from wailing to passionate reproach, and poured condemnation upon him. Louder and louder rang her voice until she was in a frenzy of excitement. Even one not familiar with the romance of the young and only sister — her flight from home, her marriage with a family enemy, the succeeding years of estrangement — could have gathered all from the broken sentences that rushed from the woman's lips as the pent-up emotions burst through at last. The death notice was the first news from the girl she had raised. And how many years had passed? She could not remember.

"Give me the letter." There was no excitement or resentment in the tones of Major Worthington's voice as he extended his hand. His calmness brought back her self-possession. She gave him the letter, and very gently, as though to a wayward child, he read it aloud, including the closing lines, which she had not stopped to decipher. It was from a minister.

"She approached the silent figure."

.

The duty devolves on me to inform you that the soul of Helen Ridgewood has returned to its God, and that to-day we have laid her body beside her husband's at this place, in obedience to her directions. She left no letter, but this message, which you will doubtless understand: "I send my child with confidence that her future will be brighter because of her mother's unchanging love for you."

The voice of the man grew very gentle as he read. There was a tone in it no one had ever heard before. Hebe gazed upon him in astonishment.

"Her chile!"

"So it seems. Now, let there be no more of this." His voice had resumed its wonted positiveness. "Put her mother's room in order," he said, drawing a bunch of keys from his pocket and selecting one, which he detached. He was apparently calm, but his hand trembled a little and his movements betrayed something of nervousness. At the door, for he had turned to go in, he stopped again.

"Isam! *Isam! Isam!*"

"Yes, sir; I 'm er-comin'." The little old man darted from behind the smoke-house, and started across the yard.

"What are you doing back there, you black rascal?"

"Ruminatin', Mas' Craffud; des er-ruminatin'."

"Well, you ruminate the saddle on my horse, and be quick about it." Then he went inside, and though the night was warm, they heard his door close loudly.

Major Worthington sent to the Texas minister, next morning, the following despatch:

Send Helen Ridgewood's child at once. How old is she? Answer.

The query was an afterthought. An exceedingly pompous young fellow, grown mighty by association with the members of the legislature and the handling of State business, took the despatch, and as he tapped with his long-pointed pencil upon the counter, and curled his slender mustache with his free hand, he said airily:

"Relative, I suppose, major. Hope it is a young lady."

"Sir!"

The feeble smile died from the young man's lips under the fierce stare of the major and the thunderous reply. He retired precipitately to his instrument. That afternoon the answer came over the wires while he, surrounded by a group of admiring and tributary companions, was explaining an invention his vast mind had conceived for the transmission of six messages simultaneously over a single wire. The answer he handed to the major read:

Helen Ridgewood will start to-day. She is six years old.

II

THE succeeding few days were busy ones for Major Worthington. He personally superintended the preparation of the long-closed room that fronted his in the great hall. The moldering furniture was removed; the moth-eaten carpet and the stained curtains gave place to new and elegant substitutes which he purchased in person. Whenever anything needed was suggested, out came the great roan saddle-horse, and off went the major to Milledgeville. Another person would have prepared a list; but that was not the Worthington method, and the results were a dozen trips. As the time approached when the little traveler might be expected, he grew more restless. Finally all the arrangements were complete. That night he slept but little. Twice he called Isam, and made him hold the lamp while he studied the situation in the child's room. Its furniture was elegant; its appointments were perfect. The smiles came and went upon the face of the old negro with more than usual rapidity, and when at length he was permitted to retire for a final nap, he muttered to himself:

"Dat chile ain' goin' ter want fer nothin'. He goin' ter mck up fer two."

Just before daybreak, Major Worthington arose
and sought the room again—this time alone. Seated
upon the edge of the bed in the less than twilight of
the place, he lived over many of the years that were
gone. Slowly, as he sat there, out of the gloom, as
the gray dawn brightened, grew a fair young face on
the wall opposite him. The eyes, frank and smiling,
were full of love, and were bent steadily upon him.
He carefully wiped the dust of slumber from his
lower lids, flourished his red handkerchief vigorously
an instant, and went upon the back porch to call
Isam.

That morning he had not more than half finished
his pipe when he suddenly struggled to his feet,
under the stimulus of an important idea. He went
at once to the room, and soon all the new furniture
was dragged out. The great mahogany bed gave
place to a tiny carved affair, resurrected in the lum-
ber-room, and off he posted to town, Isam following
soon after in a great wagon, not surprised, but merely
wondering what was coming next. He found the
major at a furniture-store, deep in the mysteries of
furnishings. He had selected a tiny bedroom set —
bureau, chairs, rockers, wash-stand, fire-dogs, and
rugs. Leaving directions for Isam to load these, and
to follow to the drug-store, he went away as fast as
the peculiar style of his own anatomical architecture
and his more than usual excitement could carry him.

The furniture-dealer asked Isam the question he dared not put to the major.

"Yes, sir," replied that worthy, with dignity; "little miss's chile comin' ter stay wid us. Nothin' but de bes' good enough fer her."

"Why, I thought the major had sworn never to recognize his sister. Did n't suppose he ever knew where she lived."

"Who tell yer dat? Some folks mighty pesterin'. Mas' Craffud know 'bout 'er all de time — all de time, an' beg 'er ter come back; but dat man she marry say no, an' she war n' de woman ter go back on de man she marry. Las' thing she did was ter send us her chile. Don' look much like dey was n' rec'nizin' one ernuther!" Isam gave the off mule the full benefit of his indignation.

"Strange how these old negroes will lie when it comes to a matter of family pride," laughed the furniture-dealer to his clerk.

When Isam reached the drug-store, the major had secured a downy little brush intended for the first hair of childhood, and a diminutive comb. Now, Isam had been ignored in these matters until his pride was suffering, and as the major was about to withdraw, he said, after searching the show-case with his keen little eyes:

"Mas' Craffud, I disremember what dey calls 'em, but de chile's ma used ter set pow'ful store by dem dere t'ings what woman-folks jab powder in deir face wid."

The major started back toward the druggist.

" Let me have the best one you 've got."

" An' de powder too," said Isam, suggestively, rubbing his chin and smiling.

" How much powder ? " asked the dealer, his voice falling into the musical tones of the negro's.

Isam bent his brow and screwed his lips together reflectively.

" 'Bout five pounds 'll do, I reck'n, Mas' Craffud — 'bout five pounds. Hit ain' goin' ter tek long ter git mo' ef dat don' hold out."

" Make it ten," the major said ; and, full of laughter, the druggist withdrew behind his desk to fill the order.

Isam was now thoroughly happy, but he was intently studying the show-case. He began again with dignity and deliberation :

" Den, dere 's de c'logne-bottles at home all done empty. Her ma never go nowhar 'dout she flip er little c'logne on 'er han'k'ch'ef."

The smiling druggist drew down a great bottle of golden fluid. A child requiring ten pounds of powder would certainly need a gallon of cologne. But Isam shook his head. "Dat ain' gwine ter do. Hit 's got ter smell er pertic'lar kind er way."

The puzzled druggist looked toward the major,

" Isam gravely smelled sample after sample."

who had sunk into a chair and with twinkling eyes was regarding the old negro's attitude.

"Let him smell all you 've got," he said, hitting the floor with his cane.

So Isam gravely smelled sample after sample, shaking his head over each. But suddenly the faint, fine odor of violets floated out.

"Dere 't is! dere 't is!" he exclaimed joyously. "Lord, Lord! but hit looks like I kin see dat lace han'k'ch'ef right 'fo' my eyes, an' her des shakin' hit in de win'."

Major Worthington started up suddenly and stood in the doorway with his back to them; but Isam calmly gathered up the purchases and loaded them in the wagon.

"All dis mighty good," said he, sententiously, as the major was moving off — "mighty good; but er chile is er chile, an' her ma used ter tek pow'ful kind ter candy."

His master looked at him in genuine admiration.

"The nigger 'll be running for the legislature," he said, chuckling.

Isam gave expression to his childish laugh of happiness as they hurried off.

"Ten pounds of mixed candy," said the major, entering a store and startling the bald-headed little old proprietor almost out of his wits.

"Certainly, sir; certainly." And he was already

journeying from jar to jar when Isam, recognizing his newly acquired rights, knocked on the show-case. He had become transformed into a fine gentleman. No lord of the admiralty ever bore himself more grandly. He extended his left hand toward the shopkeeper, motioning downward rapidly with his long black fingers.

"Don' want none er dat stuff — don' want none er dat stuff!"

The proprietor, astonished, and swelling with mimic rage, paused and looked at the negro, and then at the major, who was almost exploding with laughter.

"What have you got to do with it?" he snapped out.

"Everything!" roared the major, interposing. "Take the gentleman's order, sir. What is it, Mr. Dewberry?"

Isam pointed coolly to a box of chocolate-drops.

"Dere 't is. Her ma would n' tech nothin' but dem. I seen her tried too many times."

So the box of chocolate was wrapped up.

As they went out, the fiery little confectioner kicked the astonished cat across the shop, and boxed the ear of a little boy who begged him for a gumdrop.

Isam was now in command. He led the way into a toy-shop, and made glad the heart of the patient little woman by the reckless extent of his selections.

But the major was not to be outdone. As these things were being placed in the vehicle, a little boy came along, driving a pair of well-broken goats hitched to a home-made wagon. To him he displayed a shining gold piece.

"How will you swap, young man — ten dollars in gold for the goats and wagon?"

The boy's eyes opened wide, and Isam laughed aloud.

"I 'll ask pa," said the youngster, and with the money in hand he darted away. "All right!" he called out from the distance, coming back with beaming face and full of excitement. The goats and wagon were lifted in before he reached the scene.

"Now go home."

This was said to Isam; but he only laughed and looked down.

"Mas' Craffud," he said, "hit 's er long ways home."

"Well, sir?"

"An' hit 's mighty hot day."

"Well, sir?"

"Spec', 'fo' yer start out, better git somebody ter mek yer up one dem ole-fashion' julips." And the smiles filled his face.

"Ponder," said the major, turning to a grocer who stood looking on, "give the negro a drink."

Isam took the shining dime, and, still laughing, disappeared into the store.

III

THE Worthington family carriage in those days
saw but little service, as the saying is. Half a dozen
times, perhaps, during the sitting of the legislature
the blacks were harnessed to it, and with a dignity
befitting their score of years they trotted off to town,
the length of their stride varying not one inch in a
decade, the methodical switching of their tails never
changing, winter or summer, as it was timed to the
swing of their bodies, and sufficiently rapid to afford
an ample defense against flies. At such times they
drew back and forth some choice spirits for a game
of cards by lamplight on the broad back porch, or, if
the weather demanded, in front of the log fire within
doors, gun-wads serving for chips, and Isam concoct-
ing the famous Worthington mint-julep, which, while
it lacked the handful of hail that Jupiter first added,
nevertheless lost nothing thereby, for the deep well
registered sixty even in August. Occasionally the
old vehicle attended a neighborhood funeral, its ponderous dignity and evident aristocratic aspect afford-
ing always not a little comfort to mourning relatives.
Once a year it went to Milledgeville to meet a maiden
Worthington aunt, who swooped down at stated in-

tervals on the major's rooms and waged bitter war
with the spirit of disorder there; and once a year it
carried her back to the train, a defeated and embit-
tered woman, Isam on the box above laughing softly
to himself, and Hebe at home heaving ponderous
sighs of relief.

War buried the bolts and irons of that lumbering
old carriage in an ash-heap; but had it survived, it
would greatly amuse the new generation with its
stage-like body, much given to rolling, its broad re-
ceptacle in the rear for baggage, its airy driver's box,
and the vast expanse of cushions within. No young
person of this age could fail to be startled to see,
when the door was flung open, — a door almost as
ponderous as that of a bank safe, — the unfolding
steps come tumbling down tumultuously to the
ground, and the cavernous recess exposed. Poor old
carriage! It was an object very familiar to the
neighborhood, for in the course of its long career
nearly everybody between Woodhaven and Milledgeville had, at various times, assisted to extract it from
the ditches, while the major stood upon the nearest
elevation, and swore at Isam, horses, coaches, luck,
and the world in general.

This was the vehicle that rolled from Woodhaven
on one eventful Thursday morning, with Hebe inside
as a grand lady reclining on the cushions, and Isam
presiding above. Major Worthington had prepared

to accompany them, but at the last moment turned
back.   .

"Go on," he said to Isam, abruptly. "She 'll have
her nurse with her, I reckon. I 'm not going to ride
in a carriage with two niggers and a baby."

He climbed the steps, and resumed his favorite
seat, filling his corn-cob pipe, and paying no further
attention to the departure of the vehicle. But Isam
shrewdly suspected that the major feared to face the
crowd around the depot.

The major's chair occupied a commanding position.
He never troubled to send for any one who happened
to be within a quarter of a mile of him, and visible.
He could reach that distance with his voice without
shaking the ashes from his pipe. He was particu-
larly restless and irritable that morning, and his demands on first one and then another of the passers-
by were numerous, and took such shapes as this:
"Here — Aleck! Oh, run here and shut that garden
gate! Don't you see the goats going in there?" Or,
"You, Tom! *Tom!* Toм-м-м! Run that peacock away
from those chickens! You going to stand there and
let him kill the last one of them?" Or, "Billy! *Billy!*
BILLY! HERE! Run here and get some corn for
this hen! No; not that one — the setting hen. Tut!
tut! tut! Now look at you, you black rascal! Don't
let that turkey get it!" And so on. I need hardly
say that these sentences were garnished with certain

other phrases that had become familiar at Wood-haven.

As the day wore away he loosened his collar,—one of those old-fashioned collars that were sewed upon the garment beneath,—and drew the soft, puffy cambric shirt away from his flesh, nodded a little, and thought a great deal. In the afternoon there was heard the rumble of wheels, and presently the familiar outlines of the old carriage blocked the view at the side gate. Major Worthington maintained his position of dignity and repose, his left leg extended across the chair in front, over the back of which his arm was also thrown, his slouch-hat tilted a little against the reflection shed upon him from the pale-blue sky.

But Isam's chin was down between his shoulders, and his head wagged strangely, while in the shadowy interior of the vehicle Hebe's teeth shone like a gigantic ivory brooch in a doublet of black velvet.

Isam threw open the coach door, the steps rattled down, and the lithe form of a young lady in black, with face heavily veiled, descended to the ground and came across the yard. Paralyzed with astonishment, Major Worthington moved neither hand nor foot. Then she came up the steps quickly, throwing back her veil. A fair young face, pale with emotion, was turned to his, and soft blue eyes swept down into the past which lay buried within his heart's silence these long years. Something like a great fear seized him.

It was as though out of the old times his little sister had come, a fair ghost, to bless and forgive.

She dropped beside him, and twined her arms over his shoulders; her composure vanished, and, sobbing, she let her fair head fall upon his breast. A tremor shook his form, then two or three great soundless, tearless sobs. Raising her face hurriedly, he kissed her once upon the forehead, and struggled to his feet. Then he awkwardly lifted and supported her along the hall to her room; for her emotion was now beyond control, and he was altogether confused. But at the door of her room he paused in consternation. There were the little trundle-bed, the tiny bureau and furniture, the toys arranged to attract attention, the little baby-brush and comb, and — the candy.

"That scoundrel in town told me it was a baby!" he thundered, his excitement, by easy transition, running to rage. The incongruity of the arrangements turned the tide of her emotion also. She began to laugh and cry by turns. Putting her arms around his neck impulsively, she kissed him on the lips.

"Hebe told me — it was a mistake — sixteen instead of six. And how good of you, Uncle Crawford! how good of you!"

"I 'll horsewhip the fellow within an inch of his life!"

"Oh, no, uncle; it was only a mistake — and I am glad of it. Don't you see, it makes me feel at home already."

"She began to laugh and cry by turns."

Here they heard the scampering of feet in the hall, and the rattle of wheels; and, guided by Isam, who was bending double with laughter, ducking his head right and left as the animals pulled upon their bits, which they champed excitedly, the goats and wagon came full into the room.

"Dere dey is, little miss; dere dey is. When yer goin' ter town, hyah yo' team. Ef yer feared ter drive 'em, Mas' Craffud he git in an' hold de lines."

The major seized a chair and swung it aloft; but Isam fled, and a scream of laughter from Hebe outside mingled with the echoes of his flying feet.

Helen, smiling through her tears, soon after guided the team out with her own hands, and the old twinkle was visible in the major's eye that shone over her shoulder.

The charm of youth enveloped the old house again, and that night a mocking-bird came and sang for hours in the rose-bush at the end of the porch. If Hebe is to be believed, none ever sang there before.

THE HARD TRIGGER

I

HE news traveled fast. It swept like wild-fire over a prairie, did this particular piece of news. Major Worthington's only sister, who ran away years before with a dissolute music-teacher, and was not again heard of until now, had sent him as a dying gift her child; instead of a babe, as supposed, the child proved to be a girl upon whom the graces of womanhood were beginning to fall; she had already mastered the free-and-easy customs at Woodhaven, and order reigned at last in that bachelor stronghold.

The rumors even entered the halls of that ponderous body, the Georgia legislature, and became a ruling theme with the younger members, who posed for the gallery when not thundering away for the country upon the vital topics of the day. It went the rounds that the lady was of rare beauty, form, and culture; that in her all the accomplishments Texas could afford, such as horsemanship, lasso-throwing, and shooting, were happily blended with the graces of a famous finishing-school in New Orleans; that she could speak four languages besides that of Texas, and play the piano with her eyes shut.

Such extravagant praise grew from doubtful facts, as those who know the unchangeable old world's methods may well understand. Some of it was traceable to an old negro body-servant belonging to Major Worthington, Isam by name, who was wont to come to town on sundry errands, and was much given to discoursing on the old Worthington family.

As may be imagined, the prospect of such an accession to the cultured society of Baldwin County created a lively interest, and the etiquette of mourning, which needs must be observed, only aggravated the situation. Gradually, however, more authentic and definite information began to attach itself to the meager facts that society had gathered. A gentleman had met the lady near Woodhaven, taking the horseback exercise that her pale cheeks demanded. She was "spirituelle"; her eyes were "superb"; her sad smile was "ravishing." A lady met with like good fortune, and, emboldened by superior age and the consciousness of a leading social position, introduced herself, and gained a few moments' conversation. She found her vivacious when aroused, and her voice was "as the music in the pines." A visitor who called to see Major Worthington, some six weeks later, caught a glimpse of a delicate foot pressed against the soft pedal of the old piano; it was exquisitely modeled, and the plaintive nocturne into which the fingers strayed was as "the rippling moonlit waters in a summer night." At the end of two months Milledge-ville was prepared for anything.

One day when noon had paralyzed action of every description, from legislative to mercantile, and the doorways and shady corners were dark with idlers, the sound of hoofs smote the air, and hundreds of eyes caught the vision of a slender, flying bay mare bearing a girlish form. The close-fitting black habit reduced her figure to its minimum; into the pale cheeks had come a faint glow; the gloved hands were small. She sat her saddle so easily, so steadily, so nonchalantly, that the spirited animal seemed entirely uncontrolled as she passed. Behind her, upon the great roan recognized at once as Major Worthington's, was a little gray-headed negro incased in an old blue uniform that boasted a white heart front, and wear-ing a black chapeau of the present Knight Templar pattern. He held the taut reins with both hands, swinging far back in the saddle, to resist the holiday spirit imparted to the roan by the slender steed ahead; and when, with a slight motion, the young woman checked the latter in front of a dry-goods store, the old negro spent a few moments in the air during the roan's clumsy efforts to reduce his speed.

Milledgeville gasped, then started forward. But

the lady had gathered her skirts from the saddle-horn, leaped lightly to the ground, passed the reins to her attendant, and, looking neither to the right nor to the left, disappeared within the store. Immediately within that particular store trade was resumed actively. Young legislators strolled in. Handkerchiefs, pins, and perfumery went off rapidly, and big bills were tendered in payment; and during the changing of these, eyes that only half disguised their curiosity sought for glimpses of the fair young face. But the visitor saw none of them. She bent over some dark goods which the awe-struck clerk exhibited, and to those behind her revealed only first one and then the other soft white cheek.

This was not to continue long. At the end of half an hour a gentleman entered upon a bona-fide errand. He was tall and stately. From under his soft black hat the whitest of locks drooped and curled against the ruddiness of his smoothly shaved face, to the right and left of which stood the great points of his immaculate collar, like guards of honor. His suit was of the softest blue broadcloth, his Prince Albert buttoned at the waist, allowing the upper part to divide over a puffy shirt-front as white as the lint that falls from a cotton-gin. In his left hand he carried a ponderous gold-headed cane. He walked at once to where the clerk was displaying his goods, and asked him a question. He had not noticed the lithe little figure in black; but at that instant, as though responding to an indefinable something in the rich, courteous, sonorous voice, she turned and met his glance.

"I beg pardon, miss," he began, lifting with an old-time grace the soft hat, and leaving the beautiful white locks visible. "I did not notice—" He stopped short; a puzzled look dwelt for an instant on his genial face, then its lines straightened. "Helen Worthington!" he said involuntarily, scarcely aloud, as though in answer to an unheard question.

A wan, sweet smile crept over the girl's face. "My mother," she said softly — "my mother, who is dead."

He looked at her in confusion for a moment, then said hurriedly: "Yes, my child; I remember, I remember. So your mother is dead!" He changed his hat to his other hand with some agitation, and, drawing out his handkerchief, swept his forehead. "Forgive me! I was one of her old friends,— one of your uncle's friends,— Dr. Huger Bailey. But I am delaying your purchases," he continued, changing abruptly. "Tell him, if you please, that I have just returned from Washington, and will see him very soon. And then I shall hope to renew Miss Helen's acquaintance." He smiled genially and she gave him her hand.

For a few moments she stood watching the door. "Hujee Bailey!" she murmured. "Where have I heard that name? Why, the letter, to be sure! But that was not Hujee: it was Huger."

Dr. Bailey went to the hotel with somewhat hurried steps, his eyes upon the ground. As he entered the broad veranda he passed a group, one of whom, a heavy-set, black-browed man, was talking. An instant sooner or later, and there would have been no turning-point for this chronicle; the doctor would have passed him without pausing. But at that moment there fell upon his ear these words:

"Helen Worthington was never married; it is unfortunate for the girl."

Dr. Bailey broke through the circle and stood in front of the speaker, his face now pale, his form tremulous with rage.

"You lying hound!"

His heavy stick fell with a crash upon the other's head. The blow was half foiled by the column behind the speaker. There was a scuffle, a drawn pistol, quick action among the bystanders, and the principals were drawn apart. Speechless with rage, Dr. Bailey was forced into his room.

A few moments later one of the younger legislators was lazily causing the yellow billiard-balls to collide upon the moth-eaten cloth of the table belonging to the hotel, while his companion drew the foundations of a julep through a straw.

"What"—click!—"do you suppose stirred up the

7

old doctor so? I never saw a man get mad all over so quick." He sent the dark ball spinning around on the reverse English. "Dreadfully imprudent, this sort of weather, I should say. Your shot."

The other put aside his glass, and studied the situation of the balls with the utmost gravity as he chalked his cue.

"Friend of the family, I believe. Have heard that he was to have married the first Helen, but the music-teacher cheated him. If I make this shot, good-by to your money."

All this time the spirited mare champed her bit in front of the dry-goods store, tossing her head with impatience, and jerking the old negro's arms violently up and down. But the roan was no longer trouble-some. He had already repented. So it was that the negro gave his undivided attention to the mare.

"Des look at 'er now!" he exclaimed indignantly, as the wind blew his chapeau to the ground before her, and she plunged so violently that the old Mexi-can uniform split between the shoulders. "Whar you f'om, you ain' see nobody's hat blow off befo'? Whoa, I tell yer! Ef I had my way, I 'd put yer ter er plow — carryin' on like somep'n' 'stracted!"

Isam had restored the chapeau to his head, and the mare seemed to have just discovered the queer effect of the Mexican combination. He had a grip upon the bit-reins with both hands, and she was pulling back with all her might, snorting violently. "'Spec' ef you 'd seen Gen'l Scott you 'd er broke yer fool neck. Hit 's des like dese Kintucky folks, puttin' off deir crazy, glass-eye stock on gemmen," he continued grumbling, though the mare had quieted down as suddenly as she had flared up.

"Dainjous sort er mare, Unc' Isam; ain' fitten fer no lady ter ride."

Isam surveyed the speaker, a young hotel waiter, with disdain.

"What you know erbout er horse? Better go 'long back 'bout yo' business, an' don' be stickin' yo' mouf inter er folks' 'fairs. May be dainjous to po' white trash what raise you, but don' bother young miss no more 'n er tame rabbit."

"Dat so! I see 'er come erlong des now, an', gemini! she rides!"

This tribute to Isam's mistress had its effect. " Ef you 'd er seen 'er de day dat de drover come erlong wid dis hyah mare, I reckon you 'd er t'ort so, sho'. All young miss say uz, ' Isam, put saddle on 'er, Isam'; an' me an' Black Bill an' dat white man put de saddle on 'er. I been roun' mules er long time, but nothin' tech dis mare for cavortin'. She uz des draggin' us all roun' de yard, an' hittin' out wid dem front foots er hern like er cat, when young miss bounce up in de saddle, an' say, ' Let go 'er head.' Well, fer 'bout fo' minutes de a'r uz fa'rly full er hoofses and heelses, an' de dus' flew. Den, fus' t'ing yer know, young miss uz smoothin' down dat neck, an', bless goodness! de mare uz es tame es er houn' dog behin' de stove."

"What did de major pay fer 'er?"

Isam swept his eyes over the fine points of the animal, and looked at his interrogator hard for a moment. His voice sank to confidential tones.

"Cheap! Dat mare win ninety-fo' races in Kintucky, an' jus' goin' on five years ole. Money could n' tech 'er. But she done kill fo' men on de track, an' de jedges rule 'er off up dere. Mas' Craffud give. twelve hunderd t'ousan' dollar fer 'er des es she stan'. Whar yer goin' ter, Pomp?"

"Gwine down ter de stable ter tell 'em dat Mas' Ram Billin's ain' gwine ter want de horse he order up. Dr. Bailey done bus' Mas' Ram's head open wid er stick."

"Oomhoo!" Isam was all attention.

"Mas' Ramsey say somep'n' 'bout de young lady what ride de mare, an' fus' t'ing you know — blip! an' Dr. Bailey's stick come down on es head."

"Hush! What 'e say 'bout young miss?"

"Dunno; but 'e did n' say hit erg'in."

Pomp grinned, and sprang aside as Helen came forth from the store. She handed Isam a small package, vaulted lightly into the saddle, and turned her mare's head homeward.

II

"WHY 'n thunder don't you take the saddle off those horses, you lazy rascal!"

Major Crawford Worthington sat upon his broad back porch at Woodhaven, loading his pipe. His ample form filled the great open rocker to overflowing, and beneath his broad-brimmed hat his small eyes fairly glared.

Isam received the discharge, and passed it on. His voice was as nearly an echo of his master's as his lesser lungs would permit.

"You Bill, why n't you come git dese hyah horses? You goin' ter stan' out dere all day?"

"No; you, sir! Take 'em out yourself!"

This time the major roared, and hit the floor a thunderous blow with his ever-present stick.

"Now, uncle,"— Helen held up her finger at him as she crossed the yard rapidly toward the porch,—"you were not to swear any more before me."

He struck a match, and as it flickered above his pipe he grumbled: "That trifling scoundrel would make anybody swear."

"No; Isam is perfectly right."

"Oh, he is, is he?"

111

"Certainly.   He has on his dress-suit, you see —"

"Ho, ho!"

" — and naturally wants to preserve it.   You ought to commend rather than blame him.   Besides, it is Bill's business to attend to the horses."

"It is n't."   The major drew in the corners of his mouth, and hit the floor again.

"Yes, it is."   She was standing by him, stamping her foot.   "You have spoiled them all by the absence of system.   What 's nobody's business is everybody's business, and what 's everybody's business is nobody's business."

"You don't tell me!"   He looked up in affected surprise.

"I do," she said, laughing, and kissing his cheek.

From the far end of the hall she called back : "Isam belongs to the house, and would lose caste by doing stable-work."

The eyes of the major twinkled as he struck another match.   But they reassumed their glare at once. Isam was softly creeping up the steps, his cunning little eyes stealing sidelong glances at him.   "You black rascal," he said in a low tone of voice, throwing in a genuine old-time anathema.   But Isam merely let one of his genial, fleeting, complicated smiles flicker on his face, and followed his protectress inside.   As he passed on to the foot of the steps he affected a dispirited look.

Isam on the stairs.

"Young miss!" he called gently.

Helen came to the door. The old man fixed his eyes upon the floor, and spoke hesitatingly. "Don' you set too much sto' by Mas' Craffud when hit come ter gittin' shet er his ole tricks. He goin' ter cuss des de same when you ain' roun'."

"Do you think so, Isam?" A shadow fell upon her face.

"Ain' I know hit? 'T ain' been two minutes since he stop me out dere, an' cuss tell I 'm 'bliged ter bre'k loose an' lef' him."

"Why, I did n't hear him!"

"No, marm." Isam laughed silently. "He too smart fer dat; he git es voice 'way down. But 'e cuss des de same — des de same."

Isam resumed his journey up-stairs, but, seeing that she had returned to the porch, waited at the turn. He heard her voice in fine scorn:

"Indeed, Major Crawford Worthington!"

There was silence for a moment. Isam knew exactly what sort of face the major was turning toward her — eyes wide open, lips parted. He ducked his own head almost to the floor, and grasped the balusters in an ecstasy of delight.

"Oh, you don't understand! But you can promise your niece, upon the honor of a Worthington, that you will not curse my servants, and you do it when you think I cannot hear — lowering your voice —

practising deception. Are n't you ashamed of yourself ? "

He restored his pipe to his lips, and closed his teeth upon it. "No," he said, as he settled back in his chair.

Presently, when she was gone, he shook silently as he recalled the situation. "'*My* servants'!" he said. Nevertheless he was glad to see signs of returning cheerfulness in her voice and manner, and he realized that her system had already worked wonders at Woodhaven. Instead of being ruled by Isam and the house-women, he had only one to contend with. He fell to dreaming of the old times. "Just like her!" he said, and pulled his hat down farther over his eyes.

When Isam had returned his cherished uniform to its resting-place with the other Worthington plunder in the cedar chest in the garret, he returned to the back porch. For a few moments he stood silent, the shadowy smiles coming and going upon his black face.

The major's stout figure was comfortably adjusted to the chair, and he was smoking straight ahead. Finally he took his pipe from his mouth, and burst out with : "Well, why don't you talk ?" His stick emphasized the explosion.

"Uncle! Uncle!" Helen's voice floated out from the house, and reassured Isam. He held an enormous silver watch in his hand.

"I was des er-sayin' ter merself, ef I had er-took
my ole watch 'long ter town, an' Mas' Craffud had
er-gimme 'bout two dollars, 'spec' hit 'u'd be runnin'
now es good es anybody's."

" Does you just as much good one way as another."

"How I goin' ter tell what time ef hit ain' er-
workin' ? "

" You can't tell time when it is working."

"Don' you b'lieve er word er dat, Mas' Craffud;
don' you b'lieve er word er dat. Ole miss show me
how forty years ergo."

The major took out his open-face gold watch, and
held it in front of the negro. " I 'll give you two
dollars if you will tell me what time it is."

Isam examined the watch critically. Then he stole
a look at the sun. " Hit 's two o'clock."

The major laughed. "Twenty minutes to two,"
he said at length.

Isam put on his spectacles, and studied the figures
again, and again he stole a glance at the sun. " Dat
watch ez wrong," he said — " 'way yonder wrong.
Hit 's des two o'clock."

He never knew why the major laughed so; but
laugh he did until the tears ran down his cheeks, and
he was seized with a coughing-spell, and the delayed
dinner-bell rang.

The chances are that Major Worthington would
have smoked himself asleep in the great oaken chair,

as usual, that afternoon, and that life would have glided on in the same old way at Woodhaven, had not Isam sat down upon the back steps just at the critical moment, and, after some time spent in reflection, given expression to the thoughts that were troubling him. He spoke in a low voice:

"Dey 's done had er pow'ful row in town — Dr. Bailey an' Mas' Ram Billin's."

"Ram Billings?"

"Yassah; dey 's had er pow'ful row."

Major Worthington squared himself with the speaker. "Well, go on!"

Helen was slowly running over some old air on the piano; her warning call floated out again:

"Uncle!"

"An' Dr. Bailey bus' es head wide open wid er stick."

"Good! He ought to have done it."

"Would er killed him, mebbe, ef 'e had n' hit er pos' too, dey say."

"What was the fight about?"

"War n' no fight at all. Mas' Ram 'e up an' say somep'n' 'bout young miss, an'— blip! down come de stick. Dat settle hit."

Over the florid face of the major swept a sudden pallor, and, as though resuming the activity of twenty years ago, he stood up without an effort. His whole manner changed; his voice was grave and deliberate.

"What did he say, Isam?"

"Don' know, sah."

"Does *she* know anything about this?" He nodded his head toward the hall, and whispered the question.

The next instant Helen stood in the doorway.

"Uncle," she said, remembering her commission, "I saw Dr. Bailey in town this morning, and he told me to say that he had just returned from Washington, and would come out to see you soon."

"Dr. Bailey! I must see him immediately. Get my horse, Isam!" He passed hurriedly to his room.

Something in his face and manner attracted the girl's attention.

"What is the matter with Uncle Crawford, Isam?"

"Ain' nothin' matter wid 'im —"

"Isam, you —— black rascal!"

"What I tell yer! Young miss, what I tell yer! Yassah, I'm er-comin'." And he disappeared also.

"Don't you open your mouth about this matter while I am gone. Not a word; do you understand?"

The major's face was red, and the purple veins in his neck were pronounced; but it may have been from the exertion of drawing on his boot.

"No, sah." If emphasis meant anything, Isam was pledged, body and soul.

"I won't trust you —"

"Mas' Craffud, I ain' gwine ter talk."

"Well, then!"

"Is there anything the matter?" Helen asked the question of Isam as he passed out.

"No, marm. Des one er Mas' Craffud's notions. He wants ter see Dr. Bailey; an' when Mas' Craffud wants anyt'in', 'e ain' gwine ter wait er minute — not er minute. T'ort you done fin' dat out long ergo, young miss."

By this time he was out in the yard, and his easy laugh, floating back, quieted the suspicions of his hearer. As the major passed out she asked:

"Uncle, does Dr. Hujee Bailey spell his first name H-u-g-e-r?"

He looked at her without replying, and went down the steps.

The roan went back to Milledgeville at a pace that covered him with foam.

The legislature was sitting; but there were, nevertheless, many curious people to gaze upon the sweating roan and his portly rider as they passed along the main street and, turning, halted in front of the Bailey residence. Major Worthington advanced as rapidly as possible up the graveled walk, oblivious of the well-trimmed boxwood hedges, the clustering roses, and the warbling catbirds. The servant who met him at the door was nearly a hundred years old. No king ever wore a crown with more dignity than Reuben his age and honors. Had he not known all the great men of Georgia for sixty years or more? He bowed low, a half-smile dwelt upon his face, and the sweeping motion of his head toward the parlor door was full of grace. But it was all wasted. Major Worthington was already in the hall and looking about.

"I want to see Dr. Bailey," he said, puffing and blowing.

"I will inform him, major; I will inform him." Reuben turned toward a door near at hand; but before he reached it the major almost ran him down. The faithful old fellow made one more effort.

"I beg pardon, major. He left orders — I 'll take your name in —"

"Confound his orders! I will take it in myself." He threw the door open and strode in.

Dr. Bailey sat at the far end of the room, gazing at a note he had just opened. By him was a slender, pallid gentleman of some fifty years or less, his face clean shaved. The latter wore a frock-coat, buttoned well up, and was leaning back in his chair, slowly folding and unfolding the empty envelop. When Major Worthington's eye fell upon this figure he blurted out:

"Dr. Bailey — Colonel Thomas — this must end right here. I am the one to protect my sister's honor, my niece's name." He was hot with exertion.

Dr. Bailey had risen and taken the outstretched

hand, and had returned its strong grip. He smiled indulgently.

"Certainly, major; certainly. No man in the world is better able. But I have a separate quarrel now with Mr. Billings, and no one can take my place there — no one."

"Can't, hey! Well, who wants to, sir? Who wants to? But I claim that my grievance is older than your blow. What did he say about Helen? What was it, Bailey?"

"Crawford!"

"Don't Crawford me! Out with it!"

Dr. Bailey looked toward Colonel Thomas, questioning him with a glance. The latter had not moved from his seat; his long, white fingers were still folding and unfolding the envelop. He met the glance, and gravely nodded his head.

"Oh, well, Crawford, the fellow said that Helen Worthington — was — was — never — married —" He stopped short. The major's face was ashen. "Crawford, leave it to me."

"To *you!*" The explosion was frightful. "Leave the vindication of my sister's honor — my niece — to you — and I alive!" But instantly, almost, he was calm. "Colonel Thomas, I claim your services."

Colonel Thomas nodded; his eyes were still turned upon the envelop.

"Go to the scoundrel, and tell him that I assume

The meeting at Dr. Bailey's.

this quarrel; that as the blow was struck in the vindication of my family, I claim the right to assume the responsibility. Tell him anything! Tell him if he refuses to meet me —"

"But, Crawford —" Dr. Bailey stepped to his side, and laid his hand on his shoulder.

"I will do it! Heavens, man! Have I got to quarrel with you?"

Colonel Thomas arose; the envelop dropped upon the table.

"Gentlemen," he said,—his voice was as quiet as a doctor's in a sick-room,—"as you have both asked me to represent you in this matter, perhaps you will let me settle this preliminary question."

Both turned to him.

"Major Worthington is entirely correct," he said. "If he were to let any one else carry on this quarrel, the origin of which was an insult to his family name, he would be impeached in his honor. In addition, the political preferment he seeks would be an impossibility. No man can defend the honor of another, except up to a certain point. Major Worthington must take the lead now; and if, he having rendered satisfaction for the blow, Ramsey should still demand it of you, Dr. Bailey, you would be obligated to respond."

Dr. Bailey turned aside. He knew his friend was in the right.

"I had hoped," he said, with his back turned toward them, and with an uncertain tone in his voice, "it would have been different. I risk nothing — nothing whatever. Major Worthington now risks a great deal."

But the major had grasped Colonel Thomas's hand.

"I place myself at your disposal, colonel; only let there be no delay — not a moment."

"Then I am to understand — "

"Of course!" The major roared out the words, striking the floor with his stick. "And at once!"

Colonel Thomas understood. An authority upon dueling, he was generally consulted. When matters were left to him, a settlement or a duel at once followed.

After his second had departed, Major Worthington went over to the window. Dr. Bailey was standing there, his back turned, gazing into the beautiful Indian-summer day. The major turned him around gently, and in silence took his hand, pressed it, and would have departed, but Dr. Bailey detained him.

"Crawford, I want to speak to you — about — Helen. You would not let me years ago. The time has come now." A look of surprise dwelt upon his friend's face. "You know that she was married in Macon. Did you ever learn the particulars? I witnessed her marriage."

"You!"

Dr. Bailey walked to a secretary near by, took from a drawer a document, and passed it to his companion. The major's hand trembled as he adjusted his glasses. He looked at the doctor apprehensively once or twice before he read. It was a duplicate of the marriage certificate issued for Charles Ridgewood and Catharine Helen Worthington. Attached was the name of Huger Bailey, witness.

"I met her there with Ridgewood. She frankly told me all. It is true that she had promised her hand to me, but it was the promise of a mere girl to a man of thirty-two; her heart could not follow it. Well, it broke my heart; but she was right. I did all that I could for her, Crawford; I did all. I hurried them to the marriage. It was the best that could be done then. She might have been deceived."

A new light shone in Major Worthington's eyes; it was the glimmer of a half-formed tear, perhaps.

"No," he said gently, after a long pause, in a voice that none could have recognized; "that was not all. It must have been you who gave them money to start life in Texas. I might have done it — I ought; but it took a better man."

"Well, well, Crawford, you'll make it up with the new Helen; you'll make it up yet."

"So it was you, then? How much was it, Bailey? How much was it?"

"Crawford!"

8

" Don't Crawford me any more, 'Jee; don't do it. I am going to pay you that money. Why, did you suppose — "

" I did n't suppose, Crawford, that you would rob me of the pleasantest memory I have. Let it alone — at least, now."

There was a quaver in the doctor's voice. Major Worthington reached unsuccessfully for his hand-kerchief several times, plunged through the doorway, and, rallying from a terrific collision with old Reuben, mounted the tired roan.

III

Isam sat in the sunlight of the garret window with an open box before him. Two blue-steel barreled pistols lay in it. The old weapons had fought their way up through all the changes of modern innovation, until their original owner, Captain Vivian Worthington of Washington's staff, would not have known how to fire them. First, the cumbersome and uncertain flints were removed, a percussion-cap arrangement was substituted, and then they were sent to England to be rifled. Afterward the "saw-handles" were replaced with the round ones of this day, and double sights added. They had lain away in the old chest for full many a year; for the major's friends were all past the broiling age, and the new generation overlooked them. Once, in his silly boyhood, the major himself stood up before one of them and behind the other, on a June morning; and four white spots on his two fat legs still recorded the pathway of the compliments conferred by his antagonist.

"Dis hyah de ve'y pistol dat did de work," said Isam, picking up one of them. "Hyah de ve'y mark I scratch dere ter keep Mas' Craffud f'om gittin' front er hit de nex' time." He tried the trigger; time had made it hard to move. It was while mentally commenting on this fact that a scheme began to shape itself under the whitening wool he thoughtfully scratched.

"Dr. Bailey mus' git dis pistol," he said finally; "he mus' git dis pistol. He shoot best wid er strong trigger. Take er man wid er fat finger, an' he ain' got no business foolin' wid one er dese touch-an'-go-bang guns." He picked the other up, and examined it critically. It, too, was hard. Isam studied the situation for a long time, and then went to work upon it. "Now," he continued, "Mas' Ram Billin's he got er fat finger too, an' I 'spec' natchully er hard trigger erbout suit him; but Mas' Ram ain' no frien' er dis fambly, an' dat settle hit."

Smiling, he went to work upon the second weapon, polishing its works until they were free from rust, and oiling them until the slightest touch would bring down the hammer. Then he packed the pistols in their case, and took them down-stairs. He found Black Bill with the old family carriage hitched up, and Dr. Bailey present. The latter took the case and concealed it under his extra coat. Major Worthington looked at Isam doubtfully. That gray, gourd-shaped head, he knew, could never hold a momentous secret very long.

"Get on that box with Bill, Isam," he said; and Isam lost no time in obeying. His master was going to act as Dr. Bailey's second, and he would be present. He took his place with folded arms, the incarnation of dignity. Major Worthington kissed the brow of Helen, who came to the door.

"If I'm not back to-night, my dear," he said, "I may be gone several days."

She bade him farewell unsuspectingly, and shook hands with Dr. Bailey, who looked away from her face when he uttered the customary words of parting.

"One moment, doctor," she said, running to her room; "I have a letter for you. There," — returning,— "I came near forgetting it. I have been in such trouble and confusion of late."

When his eye fell upon the handwriting, he quickly thrust the letter into his pocket. He looked at Helen, but she had turned aside.

The carriage bore them to the depot. The next morning they were at Sand Bar Ferry, opposite Augusta, in the State of South Carolina; and a few minutes later Ramsey Billings appeared, with his young friend Albert Duncan, Esq., and a surgeon. While Dr. Bailey was conferring with the latter, and stepping off the ground, Isam availed himself of the coveted opportunity. He got close to Major Worthington, and touched his elbow.

"Mas' Craffud, Mas' Craffud, honey!" he whispered.

"Well?"

The negro's eyes assumed twice their usual propor-tions; he was on the threshold of a bloody tragedy, and of course all a-quiver with excitement.

"Listen ter me! listen ter me! Dat pistol—de one bored yo' legs—es de pistol you wanter git fer Dr. Bailey. Hit 's hard on de trigger, an' he got er fat finger. T' other pistol go off ef yer tech de handle, 'mos'. Listen ter me, honey! I 'm er-tellin' yer now."

Major Worthington looked at him curiously. "Isam," he said in a voice and manner new to the negro, "sometimes—in their excitement, you know—men shoot wild. I may be hit—may be fatally hit. You must stick to the young mistress—do you under-stand, old fellow?"

Isam was ten feet away when he finished. "Good-ness, Mas' Craffud! Whar I gwine ter stan'? Ef dey 's gwine ter be shootin' wil', lemme git erway f'om hyah."

The major could not restrain a smile; but he availed himself of the opportunity to get rid of the old fellow, who was liable to become an uncertain factor if he found out the true state of affairs in time.

"You had better get over yonder by that bush," he said. "And, remember, if you leave there it will be at the risk of your life. Whatever you do, don't come near me."

As may be imagined, Isam lost no time in following

the directions given. He took his position about forty yards to the right and rear, and awaited the end with growing excitement. He saw Major Worthington and Ramsey Billings take position opposite each other at fifteen paces, while Colonel Thomas and Mr. Duncan loaded the pistols. He could not understand why it was that his master had so little to do; but he did not fail to notice that Dr. Bailey stood beyond both, and he found infinite satisfaction in the reflection that it would take the wildest kind of shooting to put a bullet in the neighborhood of the bush. But presently, when Colonel Thomas stepped forward and took Major Worthington's hat and coat, and placed one of the pistols in his hand, Isam began to rub his eyes. Then for the first time it came to Isam that the fight was between his master and Ramsey Billings. With a cry of alarm, his eyes protruding from their sockets, he started to run around to where Dr. Bailey was standing. Just as he got well to the rear there rang out upon the crisp morning air the words:

"Gentlemen, are you ready? Fire!"

Instantly followed two reports in rapid succession, and he received a shock that sent him headlong to the ground. Had he been in a condition to observe anything further, he would have seen Ramsey Billings sink in a heap, also.

"Are you struck, major?" It was Dr. Bailey who

put the query as, in great anxiety, he advanced. But Major Worthington dashed his weapon to the ground in rage.

"The hair-trigger! Confound the meddlesome fool!"

"Keep your place, major," said Colonel Thomas, coldly. "Gentlemen, are you satisfied?" he asked the other group.

"My principal is disabled," said Mr. Duncan, rising and bowing. "The ball is through his instep."

At that moment there arose from behind the Worthington party a wail so long, so deep, so agonizing, as to chill the hot blood in their veins. Isam was rolling upon the ground, both hands clasped above his stomach.

"Oh, Lordy! I 'm killed, I 'm killed, I 'm killed!"

They hastened to his side, and Dr. Bailey raised his head.

"Where are you struck, my poor fellow? Move your hands."

Major Worthington was tremulous with excitement. "Where is it, Isam? Where is it? where is it?"

"Right hyah—right hyah! Oh, Lordy! frough an' frough! Back broke, Mas' Craffud; back broke, an' bofe legs!"

"Let me see the wound, Isam," said Dr. Bailey. "I

"'Oh, Lordy! I'm killed, I'm killed!'"

can't do anything for you while you carry on like that." He tried to draw his hands away.

"No, no, doctor! 't ain' no use. Oh, Lordy! oh, Lordy! Dere ain' nothin' but loose bones." Tears of mortal anguish were streaming down the poor old fellow's cheeks, and he was shaking as with swamp-ague.

"Isam, don't do that way. Let Dr. Bailey see your wound."

"Nothin' but loose bones, Mas' Craffud! Dey 's all broke, doctor—all broke! I got my han's on 'em."

Weakened at last, they succeeded in pulling his hands aside. No blood-stains appeared. Then the black body was hurriedly exposed; but still no injury was perceptible. Dr. Bailey put his finger into the bullet-hole he had seen in the vest. Then he began to laugh silently, hope lighting up the faces of the others as they watched him. At this moment Mr. Duncan approached them, inquiring courteously:

"Your servant, major — is he much hurt?"

"Not at all. His old silver watch saved him," said Dr. Bailey, rising, and doing his best to bring his face into a condition befitting the scene before them; for Ramsey Billings was loudly swearing at everything while the last bandage was being fastened about the wounded foot. "You understand, Mr. Duncan, that circumstances prevented my offering your surgeon any assistance."

"Confound your assistance!" yelled the pain-racked duelist, who caught his words. "But for the hard trigger you would have had your hands full. I hope I got the nigger, anyhow."

Mr. Duncan bowed stiffly. "I understand perfectly, doctor. I trust that you will take no notice of the words you have just heard. Mr. Billings is hardly responsible now."

Isam had assumed a sitting position, and drawn his old timepiece from his fob. It was indeed a hopeless wreck. Nothing could have created a reaction with him quicker than the discovery of the disaster to his cherished companion.

"Dat settle hit," he said sadly.

It had suffered often before, but all its sufferings were as nothing compared with that. The flattened bullet was embedded among the wheels, and case, crystal, hands, and face were sunk into common ruin.

The next day, as the major sat upon the back porch at Woodhaven, he handed the old fellow a new silver watch of modern construction.

"See if that keeps good time, you black rascal," he said, never looking toward him.

Words cannot describe the expression that came into Isam's face. He opened the watch, studied the figures intently for a while, and, stealing a glance at the sun, nodded his head. Then he broke into a low laugh as he exclaimed:

"Lor'! Lor'! How dis hyah watch do run! Hit 's des 'zactly nine minutes pas' eleven! 'Spec' dat julep oughter be er-julepin' 'bout now."

He laughed his little chuckle as he crossed the yard to get the mint, and at the garden gate he again took out the timepiece, studied it gravely for a moment, and, casting a sly glance back at the major, who was intently observing him from under his broad hat, called out:

"Dis watch knockin' off time like er nigger shuckin' corn. Hit 's des *fo'* minutes pas' eleven now."

There was a sudden explosion on the porch, and the fire flew out of the major's pipe as he let his merriment have full sway. And Helen, coming to the back door, laughed, too, to see him. But Isam passed around the corner with the watch, and examined it suspiciously. He found no fault there.

"Hit 's des some er Mas' Craffud's foolishness," he said; and then he gathered the mint.

Three facts in the letter which Dr. Bailey had received belong to this record.

First. The five thousand dollars sent to Helen Worthington by him were intercepted by her husband, part wasted, and part invested in cheap lands which had increased greatly in value.

Second. She had but recently gained from her husband, and upon his death-bed, her first information of the *loan.*

Third. She had by deed conveyed the land to Dr. Huger Bailey of Baldwin County, Georgia, in payment of the debt, leaving her daughter to her brother, Major Crawford Worthington of the same place.

When these two old fellows next met, Major Worthington bent his head and shuffled around suddenly until his back was turned, his hands in the meantime spasmodically exploring his coat-tails for the ever misplaced handkerchief. But Dr. Bailey, with his face brightened almost to beauty by the glow of some unutterable thought, threw an arm over his friend's shoulder, and drew him toward the window.

"I see you received my letter," he said. "What are we going to do for our Helen?"

MAS' CRAFFUD'S FREEDOM

I

EE had surrendered, and a Federal general was in Macon with ten thousand cavalrymen. The Southern Confederacy had ceased to exist.

Upon no one did these rapidly succeeding events fall with such crushing force and effect as upon that most estimable gentleman, Major Crawford Worthington, feudal lord of Woodhaven. To those who are acquainted with the major, personally or as a historical character, it is needless to state that, being at Woodhaven at the time to which this chapter relates, he occupied the familiar and well-beloved seat upon his back porch. For a lifetime, it may be said,— with the exception of his college days, his patriotic efforts to reach Mexico in time to assist at the reduction of the country in '46, a few terms of imprisonment in the Georgia legislature, and his more recent Virginia campaign,— he had virtually lived upon that particular porch, overlooking as it did his vast estate.

141

But pleasant as were his surroundings, they brought little comfort to Major Worthington. For three weeks his spirit had been greatly oppressed. Although a close observer of public affairs, the collapse of the Confederacy had found him altogether unprepared — a statement not easily accepted by those who do not know the hopeful Southern spirit. When Lee surrendered he was, it is true, appalled, but only momentarily. He felt that the South could not fail; success was certain, though how, when, or in what way, he did not know: he was no analyst. Many possibilities flitted across his mind: Johnston would retreat to the mountains, Davis would reach Texas and reorganize the trans-Mississippi department, or England would interfere. Cotton would still be king.

During three weeks, however, he had done a world of thinking. Never in his life had he thought so continuously — nay, so successfully — upon any subject, and the reaction had come.

The change came that night as he sat under the silver light of the moon. The manhood in him, so long unsummoned, so long concealed beneath that careless, easy-going, half-humorous, half-irritable quixotism, stirred under a new impulse. What it was he did not know, but he felt himself emerging from the depths, and a load lifting from his life. Light began to stream in upon him. The failure of the Confederacy not only seemed at that moment to be natural, but the only possible result. He did not realize it, but the same emancipation from exploded theory and sentimental fictions was going on from Maryland to Texas. Old gentlemen in white-oak rockers were drifting back into the Union from verandas all over the South. Wendell Phillips could no longer dare say, even in the extravagance of eloquence, that the North thought and the South dreamed. The South, which all along had thought through its politicians, was now thinking for itself.

Thus when the sound of a negro jubilee floated up from the distance it did not disturb him. He knew what was going on: a negro preacher with a smattering of political knowledge and an extensive command of disjointed but high-sounding phrases was haranguing the newly liberated slaves. He was telling them that freedom had come — that they had been "led up out of Egypt," that they had "come out of the wilderness," that their chains had been stricken from them, and that the government had promised every one of them "forty acres and a mule." They were free to select a mule each, and to mark off their land. Hence the jubilee of song and the cries of exultation; for was he not talking to children? But the older men sat with their hands against their heads, and thought. The clamor came mostly from the women and the rising generation.

As the tumult increased, the happy smile on the

major's face changed slightly. It became sardonic. Isam, who was hurrying up the steps to the porch, saw it; for at that moment above a full pipe the major held a lighted match, and Isam knew the expression meant mischief. He was suffered to get inside the back door; then the usual impatient call reached him:

"Here! Where are you going?"

"Des goin' ter wind up the dinin'-room clock an' fetch some water for Miss Helen, sah."

"What's going on out yonder?"

Isam smiled.

"Sorter preachin'-like, Mas' Craffud. Unc' Toby Johnson ez er-preachin' on freedom."

"Which side is he preaching on?"

Isam's eyes opened a little wider. He thought a moment, and then his black face lighted up:

"He's preachin' on de inside, Mas' Craffud."

The major checked a very natural exclamation when he recognized the innocent tones of the negro's conciliating voice.

"Did he tell them I am free too?"

Isam laughed silently.

"La, no, sah! Dey know *you* allus be'n free."

"Oh, they do, do they? Well, I don't; but I am free now."

"What you mean, Mas' Craffud?"

"Free from the care of you lazy rascals. I've been

pulling against it, and putting up money against it;
but now I'm free at last, and I reckon I'll say 'Thank
God!' before the year is out. Every man on this
place must look out for himself and family hereafter;
I don't want one of them. I am going to enjoy
emancipation myself until I can look round."

"How dey goin' ter git somep'n' ter eat?"

Isam's look was now an anxious one. The major
chuckled secretly when he heard "dey" instead of
"we."

"That is their affair, sir. Now *you* can get a job
almost anywhere, for plow-hands will be scarce."

"Who—me? *No*, sah; no, *sah!* I'm goin' ter
stay right hyah, Mas' Craffud. Somebody got ter
fetch water an' wood, an' wait on de table, an' run
roun' for folks, des same as fo' freedom. Ain' no use
ter talk ter me 'bout plowin'."

"Who's going to pay you? I would n't give a
dollar a month for four of you."

"Hit 'u'd be er dollar more 'n I be'n er-gettin', an'
I ain' ask no man ter raise de wages." And with a
laugh that only half disguised his genuine anxiety,
Isam disappeared.

The turmoil and disorder continued to increase
from day to day. The preachers and the women began to foment trouble. The problem was becoming
a serious one, for crops were in a critical condition,
and no contract existed between the freedmen and

9

their late owner. Major Worthington thought out a remedy at last, and one morning he turned his back upon Woodhaven, rode into Milledgeville, and boarded the Macon train. He was dressed in the uniform that he had first donned in 1861.

II

THE Federal general had found a residence suited to his taste overlooking the beautiful city of Macon nestling in the Ocmulgee valley — one of the Roman or semi-Grecian dwellings that seem to be climbing the slopes in search of the breeze. He had lunched, and was enjoying his cigar upon the broad portico, and doubtless his reflections were pleasant. The truce between Grant and Lee had been declared while he was approaching Macon with the prospect of an ugly fight on his hands. The Confederates had official information of the truce, but he had none, so he simply came in and took possession of the city, with its vast depots and supplies, without losing a man or firing a gun.

His enjoyment of the beautiful prospect framed by the massive white columns of his headquarters was suddenly interrupted by the advent of a majestic figure clad in a gorgeous uniform the like of which he had never beheld. It might have been an admiral's or a Spanish ambassador's; a marshal of France would not have despised it. As the figure approached by way of the circular drive, in the rays of the noonday sun, and with the deep-green magnolias for a background, the uniform came out in a blaze of glory.

The general rose and stood, as his visitor, sacrificing something of dignity and imposing aspect to the demands of environment, scaled the short flight of steps by aid of the hand-rail.

"I desire, sir," said Major Worthington between his breaths, "to see General ——." He saluted as he spoke; for while the gentleman addressed was very simply uniformed, he was evidently a man of rank, though just how high in position the major could not determine without his glasses, and glasses were an artistic impossibility to the regalia he wore.

"I am General ——, sir," was the reply as the salute was returned.

Instantly the major lifted his hat and bowed profoundly. "Sir," he said, impulsively extending his chapeau, "your most obedient. I am Crawford Worthington, late major in the service of the Confederate States of America. With old soldiers like yourself and me, general, the war is ended. I have the honor, sir, to offer you my hand."

The smile which was beginning to show itself upon the face of the man in blue instantly disappeared. He stepped forward, took the hand of his gray-headed visitor, and shook it cordially.

"It is indeed, major. I am glad to meet you. Will you go inside, or be seated here?"

"Here, by all means, sir. There is nothing so pleasant in this world to me, sir, as the sunlight, the blue skies, and the breezes of the South. We Southerners, sir, think it an insult to nature when a man born here needlessly turns his back on these."

"And well you may, major; well you may. How delightful they all are!" Then, quickly, "You were in the Confederate army; may I ask where you saw service, major?"

"At Manassas chiefly, sir. After that I was assigned to staff duty, and finally my State claimed me for civil service. It was hard to leave the front, but I am a State's rights man; I felt in honor bound to respond. My company, sir — the Worthington Guards —"

"The Worthington Guards! 'Gentlemen of the Worthington Guards'?"

"Yes, sir; they were gentlemen by birth, inheritance, education, and instinct, sir. Many a one of them sleeps his last sleep to-day in the valleys of Virginia." The major lifted his hat reverently as he spoke, and bowed his head a moment in silence.

The face of his host grew grave. "I have heard of the Worthington Guards, major," he said presently; "the expression 'Gentlemen of the Worthington Guards' was a familiar one in our army. I should be glad to hear more of your company. How did it happen that so small a command became so famous? How did the phrase originate?"

"Phrase? You surprise me, sir. The Worthington Guards were a company organized by myself among the best families of my county and my personal associates. They were mostly younger than myself, and did me the honor to bear my name and select me as their commander, I having had some experience in Mexico. They were all gentlemen, sir; all gentlemen to the manner born. None other could have secured admission. Nearly all of them came attended by body-servants and with large wardrobes. It took a train to move them, with servants and baggage; and not a man of them, up to Manassas, ever appeared in public except in the dress and style of a gentleman. Well, sir, as you may imagine, these gentlemen cared nothing for drill and the details of camp service. They went out to fight, sir, and, begad! they did. But they were not men to be ordered about by a social equal, sir. I would not have presumed to give orders to such a gathering of gentlemen, especially when they stood ready to grant any request I might make, and at any cost.

"Well, sir, our methods were strange to the brigade to which, over my protest, we were assigned. I thought, and still think, that we would have been of infinitely more service as a separate organization; but superior officers appealed to my patriotism, sir, and after consultation with my friends, seeing my delicate position, they yielded with fine courtesy.

"On the day of our first review the difficulty I had foreseen arose. A dapper little fellow strode out in front of the brigade, and gave command, 'Carry arms!' He was a total stranger to my company, sir; indeed, as I afterward learned, he had never been introduced to a single member, and his family name was totally unknown to any of us. Well, sir, the brigade executed the order fairly well; but the Worthington Guards remained motionless, and looked with surprise to me. Appreciating the situation, I walked out in front of them, and, guessing that the command had been authorized, I said, 'Gentlemen of the Worthington Guards, General Beauregard requests that you will bring your pieces to the position of carry.' Not a man of them refused, sir! General Beauregard afterward said that he was much impressed with their gentlemanly compliance, and appreciated the compliment very highly. He also complimented me upon my saving him an awkward situation. He did us the honor never afterward to refer to my friends otherwise than by their proper title, and they became greatly devoted to him.

"They proved their devotion on the battle-field of Manassas, a few days later. Everything was giving way on the left — hot work that, general! hot work! Bee was down, Barton was down, I was almost down, and the Georgia troops, overwhelmed by superior numbers and frightful losses, were disorganized and in confusion. It was at the time when General Beauregard, with our State flag in hand, was endeavoring to reform the line, and I was searching for him, that he said to me, 'Captain, request the gentlemen of the Worthington Guards to rally on their colors.' Sir, that was my proudest moment. I pointed out what remained of my company, then standing firm a hundred yards in advance, and replied, 'General, I have already taken the liberty to request the Worthington Guards, in your name, to remain out yonder and stop the Federal advance. If you will permit me, I will rally the colors on the Guards.' And I carried the flag to them. Beauregard never forgot that; he was a gentleman himself, and a gallant man — a trifle hasty, sir, a trifle hasty. When the fight was over he came in person to call upon the Guards. He found a dozen or so only. It was a sad day for me, general, a sad day, sir. They did not know how to refuse any request from me, and I sometimes think I made a mistake, a serious mistake."

" Battles have been lost, major, for want of a few such mistakes. I think your action was perfectly justifiable."

" Sir, your most obedient. I no longer doubt it." The major lifted his chapeau.

"And was that the last of the Worthington Guards?"

"Practically so. The company could not be recruited congenially; the members sought friends in other organizations. Only nine of eighty-nine ever returned home. But I weary you, sir."

"On the contrary, I am greatly interested."

"Sir, your most obedient." Again the gallant major lifted his chapeau.

And then, falling into conversation on the war in general, they soon reached that state of good-fellowship which makes the asking of favors as easy as the granting. It was then revealed that the major desired a detail of two soldiers to go to his neighborhood and restore order, offering his personal guaranty that they should be protected. His idea was that the presence of two representatives of the United States army would have a happy effect upon the negroes, to whom a blue uniform was an object of reverence.

"I think, sir," the major concluded, "a couple of Dutchmen will do. They won't talk too much to the hands, and they say, sir, you have them pretty fresh."

"So I have, major; and you shall have as many as you wish." He wrote two orders and handed them to his guest.

"One of them," he said, "will secure you the detail; the other will protect your Confederate decorations. You are the only man in Macon to-day who wears them."

"What!" exclaimed the major, astounded. "Is it possible? General, your most obedient. I shall continue to wear them, sir, as a compliment to you."

"Don't mention it, major; and take good care of my Dutchmen."

"Sir, it is a pleasure to meet a gentleman, even though birth has made him an enemy in war. Had you been born in this section, sir, naturally you would have been of the Worthington Guards. It is my highest compliment, sir."

The general smiled, took the arm of his guest, and gently led him within.

"Had I been born in this section I should not have been guilty of this long delay." He was filling two glasses as he spoke, and, handing one to the major, he said, lifting the other gracefully, "The Gentlemen of the Worthington Guards — the health of the living and the memory of the dead!"

The old major choked slightly over his drink, and turned away his face. His voice was scarcely audible as he took his new friend's hand and said brokenly:

"Sir, your — most obedient."

III

WHEN Major Crawford Worthington landed at Woodhaven with his two German soldiers his gray eyes sparkled and twinkled merrily. One, named Sprintz, was six feet in height, with a carriage that would have won him a place in an emperor's body-guard. His companion, Sneifleheimer, was short of stature, but made up for his deficient height by a breadth that was appalling and an officiousness that would have been unbearable if it had not been comical. The giant, on the other hand, was stolid, and never spoke except after deep reflection, his distinguishing characteristic being a disposition to agree with the preceding speaker that brought him a reputation for amiability.

The major's manner in his contact with these gentlemen was Chesterfieldian. He addressed each as " captain," and was as deferential as human wisdom could direct. All the day during their journey they had been suspiciously shy of him — in truth, not entirely satisfied as to his sincerity; but when established in a comfortable two-room house in the yard at Woodhaven and served with a box of fragrant

155

cigars and a bottle or two of old Monongahela, and when Helen, the major's niece, had inquired solicitously after their health, they surrendered at discretion. Never did broiled chicken, hot rolls, and strong coffee go home to more appreciative appetites. The major, contemplating his plan, felt that the seeds of success had been well sown, and was happy.

But seeds of trouble had also been sown. For, one morning, Captain Sneifleheimer, in the vanity of his grand title, having jostled Isam and received a dash of boiling coffee upon his neck, seized that astonished native by the collar and shook him into a panic. All that Isam could understand of the assorted language launched at him was " verdammte neegur," which he was not slow in translating into its English equivalent. From that moment Isam was at war with Sneifleheimer. He could not do enough for the giant Sprintz, although his attentions were accepted with indifference, nor too little for his mortal enemy. The result was mutual hatred and a limited race war.

Upon the morning succeeding the arrival of the military contingent the whole negro population of Woodhaven, in response to a summons from the major, assembled in the spacious back yard. It was a strange scene. Gazing down upon them from the porch were the two uniformed privates of the vast army that had set the negro free. The hands were all dressed in their best, and wore looks of curiosity or anxiety; and behind many a mother's gown were the little piccaninnies staring in awe at the "sojers," as Major Worthington delivered his first and last speech to his former slaves. He told them that the war was over, and that they were free; that freedom meant less for them,—less than they dreamed,—and much for him; that he too was free now,—free of providing for three hundred people,—and had only himself and family to look after; that, however often they had been assured to the contrary, the government would never support people in idleness, and that they must still work for their living. With those who desired to remain he would make an agreement and pay them wages, and he had brought these two soldiers representing the government to see that justice was done. They would remain as long as necessary. He did not want any man, woman, or child to stay who wished to go; they were all free, and the world was large.

When the major finished, Captain Sneifleheimer stepped promptly to the front, and waved his hand with a freedom born of natural dignity and a mint-julep.

"Yah," he said, straightening up and thrusting forward the buckle of his broad belt; " das vas all righdt, ain't it? Mejjer Verdingdon sprechen de trooth sometime already. Das vas so, Capt'n Sprintz, don't eet?"

There was a deep silence of more than a minute's duration. Captain Sprintz was standing at "carry arms" and reflecting upon the proposition. He made a military salute.

"Yah, laties und shenteelmen; das vas all righdt — all righdt," he said.

Most of the hands remained. Many of the older ones came forward with hats off, and shook hands with their late owner. Old Peter voiced the sentiments of these when he said:

"You stood by us, Mas' Craffud, an' we stood by you an' yourn too long to split off now."

For the first time in their lives they saw the old gentleman turn away, unable for a moment to speak.

But in so large a crowd there are always the turbulent and unruly, and before many days, pushed forward by their preachers and foolish women, these made trouble, and to test their new-found freedom began to loaf in the fields. Hamp Washington stopped his plow in the shade of a persimmon-tree, one day, and dropped down upon the ground.

"Look hyah, boy; what you doin'?" inquired an indignant old negro.

"I 'm free, an' I ain' goin' ter work 'cep'n' I want ter."

This produced a laugh, and a half-dozen others joined him.

"You ain' no freer 'n me," said one; and so the

little group swelled in numbers and importance until it grew to be a large group, and the work languished.

When from the porch the major saw this rebellion he almost danced. He approached the rotund form of Sneifleheimer, and, handing him a fresh cigar, said carelessly:

"I trust, sir, you have enjoyed the julep."

A grunt expressed a satisfaction for which the captain could not find English.

"Now, captain," continued his host, "we Southern people have an enormous problem to contend with; and unless you old-world people, sir, who have been through these experiences, come to our rescue with your assistance and advice, I don't know what we are going to do. For instance, sir, look out yonder. I am paying those hands wages,— large wages, sir,— and they sleep in the shade of a tree during work-hours. Now what can I do? I ask you, sir, as a business man, a man of travel and experience, how can any system of farming survive such evils?"

Sneifleheimer struggled to his feet. A string of transatlantic gutturals issued from between his lips, his bosom heaved, and his cheeks flushed. He drew around him his loosened belt, seized his carbine, and was about to let himself down the steps when the major checked him.

"No violence, captain; no violence, sir. I would prefer to lose my crop."

The soldier was indignant and irrepressible.

"I think," added the major, presently, "if you will take my horse and ride out there, your remonstrance will have a good effect."

The horse was ordered; but before mounting, to quiet the anxiety of his host Captain Sneifleheimer promised not to shoot anybody When he dashed into the startled group and cocked his gun there was consternation and a panic sufficient for a volley.

"Vadt for you tek Mejjer Verdingdon's money und sleep mid de day? Gainse sur la vork puddy quvick, und be een a hurry mid eet, or I 'll pblow oud your prains mid de gun! Hoof!"

This is about what the Africans caught from the medley; but his gestures with the gun were eloquent, and conscience has but a light task to make cowards of the newly enfranchised. In thirty seconds every plow was running.

"Oomhoo," said the old negro who had rebuked the first mutineer — "oomhoo! You fool wid dat Yankee, nigger, an' you git er bullet in your skin! Keep away f'om dem sort er folks, an' don't you put faith in nobody what talks down dey throats. When you hyah er man rumble 'way down yonder in es throat, hit 's des de same as thunder down behind er cloud. Fus' news you git, lightning 'll be er-reachin' out fer you."

And so it happened that the boys in blue rode the

fields by day, and whenever indolence sought freedom a cocked carbine stirred energy into play; and energy at play meant a negro at work. For this slight service they received the deferential courtesy of Major Worthington, cigars and spirits, and the best efforts of the culinary department. All this time Woodhaven held a spirit that laughed in silence and enjoyed life as never before. The crops were never in a more splendid condition, cotton promised to bring an enormous price in the fall, and never did slave labor toil as did the freemen under the new system.

"Begad! sir," said the major, one day, to a neighbor who was having a hard time with his labor, "keep a standing army, sir; keep a standing army. I am going to stay here and raise cotton, sir, if I have to buy some second-hand gunboats and start me a navy on the river."

Only Isam was unhappy. Poor Isam! Twice had he met the heavy boot of Captain Sneifleheimer, or, to be perfectly correct, twice had the heavy boot of the captain overtaken him, and once the angry soldier had thrown a stool at his head. To wait upon such a man was agonizing to the negro; but the major only laughed when Isam complained, and advised him to resign.

So wore the times away. The soldiers received their military discharge, but their civil appointment continued at Woodhaven with good wages. The place now had two overseers where in ante-bellum days only one had reigned. And these two in effect had the United States government behind them. The uniforms grew old and faded, but they were carefully patched and finally replaced. In place of the arms and accoutrements surrendered the major had bought others. Martial law still prevailed at Woodhaven, although it was now 1869 and peace reigned everywhere else; but between Isam and Captain Sneifleheimer there was open war.

Captain Sprintz no longer answered to roll-call. He had received a foreign letter one day, had grunted for a week, drawn his money, and disappeared.

As the major grew to be a rich man again he became tired of his system. The presence of his officious and impatient supervisor had become almost unbearable. He was weary of military occupation, and willing to get back to a peace basis even upon smaller profits. Besides, he could no longer maintain his counterfeit deference. One day Isam came up and stood by the major's chair in silence awhile, and then he said pleadingly:

"Mas' Craffud, somep'n' sorter weighin' on my mind."

"Stealing?"

"No, sah; ain't stole nothin'. But dis hyah Cap'n Yallerhammer —"

"Well?"

"Sorter looks ter me like no man got any business hittin' er child ez good as little Mas' Craffud, even if he is er sojer —"

"Hitting a child? Whose child?"

"Miss Helen's — little Mas' Craffud. Seen 'im do it wid my own eyes. Little Mas' Craffud des come up an' tech he nose wid er straw when he sleepin' out hyah, yestiddy, an' he up an' slap 'im *des* ez hard. 'Fo' Gord, I thought he done broke de po' chile's neck. But dat boy ez game: he did n' cry ner holler ner nothin'; he des pick up es little wagin an' let fly at dat white man, an' den back en de door, darin' 'im wid ez eyes des ter come inside an' tech 'im erg'in!"

"You saw him strike the boy?"

"Yas, sah; wid my own eyes. An' I 'd er bounced 'im den and dere merse'f, but he had on es barkers, an' er nigger don't stan' no chance wid barkers."

The major, who had grown pale and red in an instant, reflected for a moment or two. He knew Isam, however, and the old twinkle of good humor returned to his eyes.

"Isam," he said softly, "do you reckon you could whip him?"

"Who — me? Des lemme try him, Mas' Craffud; des lemme try him one time."

"Well, so you shall. You go out yonder while we are at dinner, and get that bucket, and sit down by the well like you had gone to sleep. I 'll get up the fight, and give you five dollars if you don't get whipped."

"How 'bout dem barkers, Mas' Craffud? I don't wanter git mixed up wid dem, ner wid de United States, nuther."

"You sha'n't; fair fight, fist and skull, and I 'll keep the government quiet. How are you going to take him, Isam?"

"Under holt, ef I c'n git hit. Ef I can't git dat, I 'm goin' ter tek what 's lef'."

"He 'll get you if you do. He is too heavy to throw. What you should do is to butt him; butt him between his eyes first, then on the belt, and when his head comes down throw your weight upon his neck. That 'll get him."

"Den des gimme time — des gimme time."

"I 'll give you all the time you want; I 'll sit right here until the army calls for reinforcement, and I 'll be slow getting there then."

Isam reflected a moment.

"Mas' Craffud," he said, scratching behind one ear a little, "I 'm goin' ter settle er heap er things dis hyah day — some er yourn an' some er mine an' all of little Mas' Craffud's; but sometimes things sorter don't work out 'zactly right, an' ef hit so happen ter-day you c'n come right erlong an' break up de fight."

The major's laugh had so much of the old-time heartiness in it that Isam more than smiled as he moved off.

Now, no greater injustice could be done to Isam than to accuse him of being brave: he was not; but he was knowing. He depended upon his enemy's surprise, corpulence, and shortness of wind for the victory. Moreover, by a little here and a little there and close observation he had formed a very nearly correct estimate of the man he was to fight, and he was no longer afraid of him when the terms were anything like equal.

Captain Sneifleheimer was a man of habit. When he entered the dining-room he always unbuckled his belt and dropped it, pistols and all, upon the hall table, to be resumed only after he had dined and smoked.

Dinner was over, and the captain was just drawing his cigar when he was startled by a vigorous exclamation from the major, who had laboriously sunk into his chair, the very manner of his sinking suggesting the cruelty of any necessity that compelled him to rise again. The captain glanced out into the yard to the well-house; there sat Isam asleep, the empty bucket by his side.

"That," said the major, "is what comes of freedom. That negro has n't been worth his salt since '65. I wish to the Lord somebody would thrash him. He needs it."

Sneifleheimer scrambled down the steps, picking up a buggy-whip as he went, and hurried, if such corpulency could be said to hurry, across the yard. He gave Isam one blow, which, asleep though he seemed to be, he shrank from in advance, and which acted as a fine stimulant to the negro's ebbing resolution.

"Gid oud, gid oud mid your schleep up!" shouted the assailant, and lifted the whip again. But it did not descend. With one leap Isam had him by both ears, and was soon jumping up in the air, butting him between the eyes. The third time Isam butted, the major's heels went over the balustrade, and he literally wallowed with mirth in his chair. Isam lost no time; the enemy was now stunned and almost unconscious, and suddenly Isam backed, lowered his head, and rammed him about the waist-band with terrific force. He did not have to jump on the enemy's neck; Sneifleheimer fell like a decayed pine. In an instant the negro was upon him, full of the memory of insults and oppressions and the mad excess of victory. He gouged and beat and clawed and pulled until the major scrambled out and drew him away.

It was known at once that the captain would have to resign; any one that Isam could whip would have but small influence. Even Sneifleheimer himself grasped the situation correctly. And so it was that one summer day the slanting rays of the setting sun gilded the patches upon a worn and faded uniform the back of which was toward Woodhaven. The United States army was retiring from Georgia.

THE WOODHAVEN GOAT

AJOR WORTHINGTON was smoking his pipe upon his broad back porch at Woodhaven, and dozing in the balmy air of a faultless morning in May. His stout form was, as usual, spread over two chairs and the balustrade, and contentment rested upon him. Well might he be content. His broad fields were already ribboned with the pale green of young cotton, and all hands agreed that the "stand" was perfect. Peace reigned at Woodhaven, after many days of disquiet, and for all he had been once a man of war, no man at heart loved peace more than did this eccentric old planter. He had tried many experiments; he had run away and marooned with Isam in slavery time, had fought a duel before the war, and had bravely worn the gray as commander of that renowned organization, the "Worthington Guards." When the unequal contest was ended, he had employed two of his conquerors with guns and blue uniforms to oversee his place, and with such success that prosperity smiled upon him. All of which is now a part of the history of his country. To-day, the day of which the chronicler is called upon to write, no cloud dimmed the horizon of Crawford Worthington, late Major C. S. A., and still master of Woodhaven. But it was to be an eventful day. Isam was in the yard, under a broad elm, sitting on the well-swept ground and busy cleaning the Worthington case-knives on a soft brick — an immemorial custom. His little black eyes, set deep within his wrinkled, complicated face, reflected the light flashed up by the polished steel, and he hummed softly a line from the old song, " My Gal 's er High-born Lady."

Over in the orchard, at the far end of the broad back yard, an aged goat was browsing phlegmatically in the fence-corners, and near the triple rows of bee-hives that were terraced upon plank shelving close to the back yard a strutting turkey-gobbler drummed among his wives.

From time to time the goat ceased to chew, and looked curiously upon the proud fowl. Possibly he wondered how anything could be so small at one moment and so big at the next. Possibly he was wishing that this same swelling gift were his; for out in the grove there lived a gigantic ram, a bitter, uncompromising foe, and the conflicts always ended disastrously for the whiskered champion, mainly, however, because he had never been able to meet his antagonist under any recognized rules of the ring, his own inclination being to spar, and the other's to ride a tournament. Suddenly, as he gazed and reflected, every feather on the gobbler fell into place, the whole arrangement closing like Venetian blinds, and the fowl, dropping his head close to the ground, struck the back of it with first one and then the other foot. Then he hopped about six feet, and lifted both wings, again ducking and scratching his head. This he repeated rapidly, his wives joining in the gymnastics, and uttering sharp, crisp clucks. Presently the whole flock scattered in a panic, ran with lowered heads to the limit of the orchard, rose on wing, and sailed away into the cotton-field.

The goat looked on this performance with great interest, until the last gray form had settled and passed from sight. He even uttered a queer little laugh that shook his whiskers. Evidently, however, the oddity of it all soon began to appeal to him, for he looked back inquisitively to the place from which his late associates had departed, his unwinking, glassy eyes full of amazement. There was no explanation in sight, nor was any suggested when he calmly went there and examined the locality more carefully. He did not even find one in the sky above, although he searched in that direction with equal deliberation.

It was while making this final survey that his attention was attracted by the low-hanging branches of a cherry-tree, deep green their verdure and seemingly succulent their leaves. He dismissed the turkey puzzle, and standing upon his hind legs, beckoned to the leaves with his long, flexible lip, a mute invitation that bore no results whatever. Jumping upon a lower hive, he rested his feet upon one above, and again strained his whole frame toward the aërial pasture. Then he mounted yet higher, and with his hind feet upon the topmost hive and his body perpendicular, reached the coveted prize.

It was at this moment that Isam, suspending work, fixed his eyes upon the picture, and keeping them there, began to feel about for the knives. His low, earnest voice broke the stillness:

"Mas' Craffud! Mas' Craffud!"

"Well?" The major mumbled the response from mere force of habit, his eyes still closed.

"Dere 's gwine ter be trouble hyah, sho'ly. Ef dere 's anyt'ing 'twix' you an' de back do' up dere, better move hit —"

"What are you talking about, you black rascal? Get up from there!"

"Mas' Craffud!"

"Get up, I tell you, and open that gate! Don't you see Jerry coming with the plow?"

"Mas'—"

"Get up!" the major thundered, and reached for his stick.

Isam darted to the gate and opened it. Jerry was on the way to plow the orchard, and the way led through the yard. Any attempt to continue the interrupted warning would have been useless, for the major discovered at that moment that the mule had been geared wrong.

"Put that back-band hook down lower, sir!" he shouted to Jerry. Jerry was excited by the old man's temper, and a natural awkwardness was against him. "Lower yet! *Lower!* Now shorten those traces! The next link! The next! The *next!* I tell you — the *next!* Don't you see you are going the wrong way? *Shorten* the chain — *shorten! shorten!*" Down went the chairs, and out came the major in a towering passion. He jerked the traces right and left, Jerry changing places with him about the pensive mule. Isam uttered a low cry and began to edge away. The goat, reaching too high, had upset the hive on which he stood, and sliding backward down the terrace, had carried several more with him.

A moment the surprised animal stood waist-deep in bees; then suddenly an electric shock went over him. He shivered, bit at his flanks, his hind leg and hip; then he jumped ten feet, and, if Isam's account of the tragedy may be accepted, swore a great shrieking oath as he began to make a rapid tour of the orchard. Round and round the goat went, praying, cursing, and crying, the crouching negro in the yard watching him with straining eyes through the picket fence. The major's attention was arrested. He looked at the negro and then at the goat.

"What ails him, Isam ?"

"Say yo' prayers, an' say 'em quick, Mas' Craffud, fer ef dat goat come dis-er-way ter git shet er es mis'ry, dere 's gwine ter be trouble." He was edging away toward the kitchen as he spoke.

"Stop !" thundered the major. "What 's all that stuff you are mumbling ?"

"Pray fer him ter find er low place inter de cotton, Mas' Craffud. Listen at dat ! Don' you hyah 'im callin' you, honey ? 'Mas' Craft-t-t !'" And Isam gave an excellent imitation.

The major did not have time to finish a laugh. A few scattering bees from the wrecked hives struck into the little group, and the mule, being the largest enemy, first received their attacks. He responded by launching out with his heels as fast as he could pick them up and put them down, gradually turning in a circle and becoming involved with the plow and lines. Presently he made a rush for the gate, and finding it closed, started on a wild career around the yard, gathering bees as he gathered momentum. Woodhaven for the time being had been converted into a two-ring circus. The goat, with his horns laid on his back, had the orchard, and the mule the back yard.

As the mule came round, the excitement increased, for the plow was swinging out on the chain-traces, knocking over benches and tubs, skinning the shade-trees, and thundering against the weather-boards of the buildings. Cut off from the porch, and driven from tree to tree by the plow, the major grew desperate. The detached kitchen, built on brick pillars, was the nearest shelter. Seizing an opportunity, he rushed to it, dropped on his knees, and crawled under just in time to escape the plow, which swept away the last vestige of the steps. Jerry had dived over the outer fence, and was viewing the drama from a constantly increasing distance.

No one responded to the major's stentorian commands to open the gate. Most of them were delivered at a disadvantage, for his head was bobbing in and out as the flying plow and his efforts compelled; but they were loud and fierce enough to be heard half a mile. When he began to call Isam, in particular, a groan behind him drew his attention, and looking back, he saw the whites of a pair of eyes gleaming in the shadow. A mighty and elaborate imprecation begun at that moment was never concluded. The goat came over the orchard fence, with a foot of space between him and the palings,— a comet from Capricornus, with ten thousand bees for a tail,— and after one frantic round in search of relief, dodged the flying plow and went under the kitchen. It was this circumstance that interrupted the major's efforts to do justice to Isam's utter worthlessness.

When the goat went under the kitchen, the major retained his presence of mind, and Isam lost his. The former, knowing that bees, when angry, follow a moving object, fell upon his face, shielding it with his arms. Isam, on the other hand, rolled out from the dark corner into the yard, and was knocked over as often as he attempted to arise, which was as often as possible; for to the infuriated goat all things were now explained: Isam was the cause of the dire disaster in which he had become involved. Therefore he fairly leaped in the air, and delivered his blows with a savage energy which would have proved fatal to any one except an African. Isam got his enemy by the horns and tried in vain to hold him; but there were no rests or breathing-spells — the bees attended to that. The man and the goat rolled over, half rose and fell, and mingled their voices like warriors of old engaged in deadly combat; but Isam's was not a defiance. In his dark hiding-place, the major, lifting his face a few inches, looked out through tears with a sudden delight at the negro's predicament, sobbing and choking with his emotion. When he heard the cry, "Help, Mas' Craffud! Run hyah, Mas' Craffud!" he frantically beat the dry soil about him with his fist for some moments.

"Better for one to die than two; it's a long sight

"There were no rests or breathing-spells."

better," the major shouted when he caught his breath. The memory of the famous conflict with the deer in the swamp had returned to him. And then he added: "Stick to him, Isam, stick to him!"

"Run hyah, Mas' Craffud! Help me turn dis goat loose!"

There was a sound as of a man choking to death under the kitchen; and then between many sputterings and coughings came a hilarious shout:

"Don't cuss, Isam, don't cuss! If ever a man had a call to pray, you've got it now. Stick to him, Isam, stick to him! Whoa, goat! Whoa, goat! Who-ee!" The major fairly rolled over on his back, and kicked the kitchen floor above him until exhaustion overcame him.

The fight outside was not as long as the memorable one with the deer. Covered with bees, man and beast broke away and disappeared from the scene. The mule had crushed down a panel of the fence, and the goat passed through the gap like a flash of white sunlight. In the grove he met his hereditary enemy, ready for a tournament. He only shed a couple of quarts of bees on him and passed away, leaving the ram to start a circus of his own, which he immediately proceeded to do.

Helen, who had made several brave efforts to go to her uncle's rescue, only to be driven back indoors, finally found the air outside clear enough of bees to permit her to approach the kitchen. She kneeled there and looked under.

"Uncle — Uncle Crawford — where are you?"

She saw the old man still stretched out under there, sobbing like a child recovering from a fit of crying.

"Don't," he whispered, pushing a hand back toward her and keeping his face averted — "don't speak to me! I am just grazing apoplexy —"

"But where is Isam, uncle?"

The portly form writhed in a sudden convulsion.

"*Don't*, I tell you!" he thundered. "Tell me something sad—tell me bad news. Go away—go away!"

Helen obeyed the final command. After a while the major crawled out and came limping across the yard. Helen covered her face and turned away suddenly.

"Don't, my child, don't!" he pleaded. "If I laugh standing up, I'm gone. What? Can't find Isam! Why, I hear his voice —"

"I do, too, uncle, but we have searched high and low in vain for him."

"Nonsense; he can't be far away if we can hear him. Find him; he must be badly stung, to say nothing of —" He stopped and pressed his sides, while he clenched his teeth.

But Helen could not find Isam. That plaintive, pleading voice seemed everywhere, and the owner nowhere. It was as though all of him had been lost but voice, and go where she might that seemed to recede.

The mystery was at last solved. A negro came into the yard for water. Presently he cried out in amazement. "Dah now! Laws-a-mussy! Hyah he, Miss Helen — hyah he down in de well!" And so it was. The desperate man had performed a very timely although very perilous feat. Maddened with pain, covered with bees, and fleeing from the face of the awful goat, he had leaped upon the well-curb, grasped the chain, and rattled down into the cool waters. He was triumphantly hauled up again; but he refused to leave his place of refuge until assured that the war was entirely over. A little vinegar and soda soon restored him to his usual size.

It was many weeks before the goat could be tolled back into the yard. He would approach within three hundred feet, point his whiskers at the house for five minutes, and then go sadly away. But Isam never could, afterward, pass him in safety without a club.

One day however, the hungry animal came gingerly into the yard and accepted some cabbage-leaves from the cook. Unfortunately, little Henry Clay had tied a string to a leg of one of those iridescent beetles commonly called June-bugs, and released him to hear the "zooning" noise of his wings, so pleasant to the ears of Southern children on a plantation. The beetle made one rush for liberty, reached the end of the thread, and curved past the goat's ear with the speed

11

of a rifle-ball. Have goats memory? It is likely. This goat went through the fence, taking six palings with him, ran headlong into a horse-stall, and hid in a dark corner. He came no more to the house.

"I know des how dat goat feel," said Isam, in describing the incident to his Miss Helen: "fus' time de chile zoon dat bug erroun' me, I was half-way ter de well 'fo' I cotch mer bref. An' dat 's er fac'."

CAPTAIN ISAM

HEN Helen Worthington's husband laid down his life for the Confederacy, gallantly leading a company in the Twenty-fourth South Carolina, and Helen had gone back to Woodhaven, Isam, who had attended his young master from Manassas to his grave, was allowed to attach himself to regimental headquarters. The colonel of the Twenty-fourth was cousin to Major Worthington, and urged the arrangement. Despite his shortcomings, the smiling little negro easily won his way to favor wherever his fortunes carried him. The major's concession was greatly to Isam's liking, for the free-and-easy life of a body-servant in the army admirably filled the demands of his restless nature; and let it not be forgotten that in camp and country there were perquisites.

Isam's duties and inclinations made him a man of peace; but in an evil moment, spurred on by his own narratives of the deeds of valor performed by himself with the famous Worthington Guards at Manassas, he actually sought service of an active and dangerous character. And thereby hangs a tale.

I

It was just before the battle of Chickamauga that Isam tendered his services as a soldier and commander to the Southern Confederacy. His black face shone with military ardor as he stated his proposition to the colonel commanding the Twenty-fourth South Carolina.

"You see, Mas' Alec, hyah ez thirty-two niggers waitin' on folks in dis hyah camp, holdin' hosses, cleanin' brasses, an' cookin'; an' hit don' look right fer dese lazy rascals ter be er-settin' roun' while fightin' 's goin' on, an' dey bosses out yonner somewhar, reskin' dey lives ter keep 'em fum bein' stole an' runned off by dem Yankees. I be'n er-drillin' an' er-speechin' ter de crowd tell dey-all says ef Isam 'll lead de way dey 'll go anywhar ter he'p dey white folks. An', Mas' Alec, ef you 'll des gimme de guns an' tell Isam whar you want de nex' fightin' done, you goin' ter hyah good news fum dat crowd. Dey means business, sho' !"

"Do you think you could hold them together, Isam ?" asked the colonel, lazily, as he refilled his pipe. "My observation has been that the boys are not fond of the smell of powder."

182

"Hol' 'em tergedder! Who? Me? Huh! Dey don' need no holdin'! Did n' nobody have ter hol' me in Virginny. White folks don' put much faith in er nigger when hit come ter fightin', but dere 's where dey ez wrong. Course er nigger don' want too much crowdin', an' all you got ter do ez ter gi' him elbow-room, an' he 'll stay 'long wid de bes' white man in de yarmy. An' dem niggers back yonner ain' no common stock; dey ez all quality, an' seen heap er 'speriunce, an' ain' nair one of 'em goin' ter run off an' leave Isam. I 'd kill de fus' rascal dat turu ez back. Des you gimme guns ter go roun', an' erbout five loads ter de man; dat 's all you got ter do."

The colonel said he would see about it, and went off laughing. But that evening the matter was mentioned at headquarters, and received favorable notice. Much to the delight of Isam, he received his guns and thirty rounds of ammunition.

"What all dat powdah an' shot fer?" he asked dubiously, as the ammunition was being distributed.

"For your men, of course," said the colonel. "You don't expect to go into battle without ammunition, do you?"

"No, sah; but hit 'll tek er long time ter shoot all dat up, Mas' Alec, an' ef you got any use fer hit down de line, I reck'n erbout five loads all roun' will do fer my crowd. Er nigger loads mighty slow when he gits de 'citcment on 'im." But the protest was unavailing.

For a week Isam was in his glory. A second-hand uniform from a general's tent, a battered cap with a feather in it, a pair of cavalry boots much worn, and a saber completed his outfit, with the exception of a huge horse-pistol, which he wore in his belt. The uniforms of his command consisted of whatever could be begged about the camp. For side-arms a few carried pistols, and more than one had hatchets. Just how many razors there were it is easy to guess, as most of the command were accustomed to shave their masters.

Isam's drilling of this motley crowd was unique, and for several days afforded the soldiers no end of fun. Day by day he grew in importance, and by the morning of the battle he was a bigger man than General Bragg, in the estimation of himself and his dusky followers.

When that eventful day dawned, Isam got his men together, and waited near the wagon-train for the orders which were to place him in the path of glory. He endeavored to explain military tactics to his command by drawing lines of battle in the sand, and indicating with the end of his scabbard the probable position of the two armies, and how movements would be effected, but with little or no success, for reasons not difficult to conceive. It was while thus engaged that a mounted officer rode up and ordered him to advance with his company, and to take position on the right of the Twenty-fourth South Carolina.

"Hurry forward," said the officer; "the fight has begun."

"I knowed dat 'fo' you come," said Isam; "dem nail-kegs[1] be'n flyin' roun' hyah thick ez bees 'bout er hive. Which way you say we mus' go, boss?"

The officer pointed to the line again, urging the new commander to hurry. Smoke was rolling upward in the direction indicated, and the roar of cannon and the rattle of musketry at that moment grew thunderous and deafening.

"Yes, sah," said Isam, reflectively; "you wants me ter tek dis hyah comp'ny, an' go up yonner by de Twenty-fourf? Did Gen'l Bragg send fer me hisse'f?"

The officer, struggling to quiet his excited horse, divided his maledictions between the animal and the anxious negro.

"Dat's all right, boss; dat's all right! Hit won' do ter git in dar, an' nobody 'sponsible. I ain' erholdin' back 'cept ter hit de right place at de right time. Is dere anybody up dere to 'splain de battle ter we-alls?"

"You won't need any explanations, man! Load and fire upon the enemy, just as everybody else is doing. You must n't waste time here. Get your men under way!"

"Yes, sah; dat's what I 'm goin' ter do. Boss, when we gets dere an' goes ter fightin', ez hit 'g'inst

[1] Large shells.

de rules ter tek res' an' shoot? Some er dese niggers can't hit er mount'in ercross er hog-pen 'lessen dey teks res'. Ef dey can't tek res', 'spec' er heap er Gen'l Bragg's powdah an' shot be wasted right dere dis mornin'."

"Confound your rest!" shouted the exasperated officer. "Get your men in line, and obey orders, or General Bragg will have the last one of you shot!"

"Yes, sah; dat 's what I 'm goin' ter do right dis minute. Fer Gord' sake, niggers, why n' yer git inter line, an' don't keep dis hyah white gemman talkin' esse'f ter deaf? Boss, ez we got ter cross dat new groun' ovah dere? 'Spec' ef you lemme tek 'em roun' frough dem woods, I could sorter hol' 'em ter-gedder."

But the officer had left in despair.

"Take them straight across to that big pine," he yelled back.

Isam looked sadly after the vanishing form, and felt exceedingly lonesome. Suddenly, however, he drew his great saber, and the fires of war blazed in his eyes.

"'Tention, soldiers! You, Pomp, git back in line, an' let dat hammer down! You goin' ter keep pro-jeckin' roun' hyah tell you shoot somebody yet! Now des look at dat yaller nigger down yonder—done lef' es ramrod en es gun! Nigger, ain' you got sense 'nough to know you can't get dat ramrod back atter hit 's be'n shot! You think you goin' ter have time ter run out 'mongst dem dead Yankees an' hunt dat ramrod? Talk ter me now; I 'm er-askin' you er plain question erbout de man'l of arms. An' dere 's Buck done got es hat on hind part befo', wid de fedder p'intin' back like he already done started out er de fight! Now y'-all listen ter me while I talk sense. We got ter go inter dis hyah fight sho', an' dere ain' no back-down en me. Berry Bowles ez de bigges' an' de fus' man in de line, an' he mus' lead de way an' y'-all des foller right erlong en es tracks. Berry, you mek fer dat pine ovah yonner on de ridge, an' I 'm comin' 'long berhin' de las' man; an' de fus' nigger what bre'k ranks ez got me ter run ovah 'fo' he leave. I done gi' y'-all fair warnin'; an' ef anybody git dis sword stuck frough 'im, ain' my funer'l march!"

Isam's command had not reached a point a hundred yards away when, back by the wagon-train, a caisson blew up. There is no telling what would have been the result so far as the reserves were concerned; but as they wavered, Isam picked up his sword, which had dropped to the ground, and shouted, "Halt!" The line steadied, to find the captain on his knees.

"Come down! come down!" he cried. And there upon the margin of that bloody battle-field he lifted up his voice in thankfulness for their escape from a horrible death, and in appeals for a continuance of divine watchfulness. Gradually as he prayed the bodies of

the negroes began to sway and their voices to blend
in a wild chant. Soon the meeting developed into a
mighty revival, and the plantation hymns rolled forth
to the strangest accompaniment ever known to African worship — the shrill fife-notes of the Minié ball
and the deep diapason of the flaming cannon. The
end came when the same officer dashed into the midst
of them, pistol in hand, and, in a tone of voice that
showed parleying would be fatal, ordered the company to advance. It advanced.

II

THE broken regiments of the Confederacy were in camp a few evenings after this eventful hour in the life of Isam, and a number of officers were discussing the situation, when Isam, coming around a tent with an armful of wood, found himself in their presence. The colonel watched him busying himself about the fire and preparations for the evening meal, and with a motion to his companions, as the darky was moving away, asked carelessly:

"Where is your uniform, captain?"

Isam pretended not to hear, but presently, when the question was repeated, looked up.

"Me?" he asked.

"Yes, you. That is Captain Isam, I believe, is it?"

"Hit sho'ly ez me," said Isam, simply.

"Well, captain, I did n't see much of you in the fight. How did the boys behave?"

"Po'ly, Mas' Alec, po'ly. Dey behave po'ly."

"Did you get up on the right of the Twenty-fourth? I sent you orders twice."

"Well, not eszackly, Mas' Alec; not eszackly."

"Go on!"

Isam looked around the circle of laughing faces, and straightened up slowly.

"You see, Mas' Alec, hit all come of dat new groun'. Ef dey had lemme go roun' frough dem woods, hit 'd er be'n diff'unt." He looked about for some way to illustrate his position, and his eye fell upon the head of a little negro girl who stood by with her empty biscuit-basket on her arm, her hair divided into little sections and plaited. " Come hyah, sissy, whar de white gemmens c'n see yo' putty head. Right up dere," he said, passing his finger along one of the shining division lines on her head, " ez whar de paf run 'cross de new groun', an' hyah ez de woods out hyah on dis side." Straightening up one of the little kinks, he continued : " Dis ez de pine-tree whar we was aimin' ter git; an' ef we had er come roun' frough dem woods, nobody could n' seen us. Out hyah was de Twenty-fourf whar dey ought er be'n, an' des berhin' dis patch er hair was de Yankees. Well, sah, de break come right hyah en the new groun'. Berry Bowles was er-leadin' de way, an' I was er-headin' off stragglers berhin', when bang ! an' one er dem nail-kegs hit erbout seven foot fum Berry, an' plowed er furrer right down 'side er de whole line, des like hit was er-beddin' up fer cotton, an' hit flung dirt on ev'ybody. Dere war n' no holdin' dem niggers den. Dey runned ober me, an' 'fo' I knowed what my name was, de groun' was full er guns an' tracks. I got on top er stump an' hollered loud ez I could holler, an', 'fo' Gord, de ouliest nigger en sight was Berry, what done fell over er log, an' was des layin' dere prayin' fer somebody ter tell es Mas' George ter sen' de doctor quick. I knowed dere war n' no use er my stan'in' up dere fer fo' thousan' Yankees ter be shootin' at, an' I got down an' went 'long back, sorter singin' ter merse'f ter let folks know I war n' anxious ter leave. I called ter Berry when I lef', speakin' cheerful-like ter calm him. Says I, ' Come on, Berry; hit 'pears like we ain' no manner ercount out hyah, an' we ez back yonner. Better step back wid me an' cook supper.' But Berry was des dat pluralized wid fear .he can't hear nothin'. So I tell him I send de doctor ef I see 'im, an' I step back by merse'f ter find my niggers. Yes, sah; I found 'em. Dey was all down by de waggins whar dey come fum, an' ev'y man tellin' er speshul lie. Well, sah, I ordered an' I begged an' I prayed ter de crowd, but war n' no use. An' den hit come ter me dat ev'y nigger dere was worf er thousan' dollahs, an' some er dey marsters was po' white men, an' could n' 'ford ter lose er nigger. So I said I reck'n Gen'l Bragg an' Mas' Alec done look atter dat little bunch er Yankees out en front, an' I better stay back dere an' keep dem niggers an' waggins fum bein' runned off. An' dat 's what I did. De white folks dey los' er pow'ful sight er stuff dat day, but dey did n' los' nair nigger, an' dey did n' los' nair waggin. Yes, sah; if y'-ll des set right whar yer settin', de coffee be 'bout right, time I come back wid de cups. An', sissy, you run 'long home an' tell yo' mammy dere 's be'n er battle took place on top yo' head."

And the man who saved thirty-two thousand dollars' worth of negroes and a wagon-train at Chickamauga disappeared under a tent, and pretended that he did not hear the laughter on the outside.

THE GUM SWAMP DEBATE

T was a gala night at the Gum Swamp Meeting-house, for the vexed question which could "argify" best — the Rev. Elijah Williams or Mr. Ike Peterson — was to be definitely settled by a public contest. It is true that the ostensible object of the meeting was to debate this proposition, " De pen am more pow'ful dan de powder," but it was recognized by the whole congregation that the real issue was as first stated.

For many years 'Lige had held undisputed possession of the pulpit and forum, and swayed his audience with homely eloquence, his logic irresistible, his facts unassailed. He had been authority on all questions, settling family as well as doctrinal disputes. If there was a mooted point in Scripture that 'Lige had failed to clear up, it was because the point was fortified behind an array of words that no one in Gum Swamp could spell out. But one day that nineteenth-century product, a " school darky," by the name of Ike Peterson, had made his appearance and begun to talk out in meeting. Ike had just enough learning to spell out the parts of the Bible he already knew, and carried in his excellent memory a jumble of facts and phrases that had stuck to his impressionable mind. But he had in addition an intense desire to be heard upon all questions, coupled with an assurance simply overwhelming. He it was who proposed th question as above, and assumed to defend the affirmative. As may be supposed, this newcomer was a thorn in the side of the preacher, and the situation was not helped by the fact that the giddy young sisters showed a disposition to cackle when he crowed.

On the memorable night of the contest Ike arose to begin the debate. Every seat was taken, and the walls of the log edifice were lined with eager listeners, while bouquets of ebon faces clustered at the open doors and windows. The speaker was at his ease, and glaring about him, said loudly:

"Huccum all you niggers hyah? Das de fus' an' fo'mos' quesshun. Huccum yer hyah? Was any uv yer blowed up wid powdah an' fell back hyah en Gum Swamp?" Ike smiled until his mouth seemed an arched vista lined with headstones. The congregation responded with a laugh. "No," he said confidentially, "ain't none uv yer been blowed up! White man tuk er pen an' writ down on er piece of paper, 'Sen' me er hunderd niggers.' An' he pass hit erlong to er ship-capt'n, an' de ship-capt'n he pass hit erlong 'cross de water to er missionery, an' de missionery he

"Ike smiled."

call up er lot er de bes'-dress' niggers in Afferca, an'
sen' 'em erlong back by de man what fotch de note.
Das how dey got de seed uv de fus' niggers, an' fum
dat start all de res' done growed tell de woods ez full
uv 'em. Hit was de pen did it. De pen ez de daddy
uv ev'y nigger in Gum Swamp." There were several
vigorous assents, and the speaker continued: "But
de white man what sen' fer dem niggers owned 'em
all, tell Mr. Linkum come erlong an' set yer free. An'
how did Mr. Linkum set yer free? I want all you
niggers what never read nothin' to git dese facts fum
me! How did yer git free? Why ain't yer all back
home yonner er-sleepin', so 's yer c'n outwalk er mule
all de week, 'stead er bein' hyah ter-night an' in town
all day Sattyday? You young niggers out dere by de
do' wid yo' moufs open, I want yer ter listen ter me!
I 'm talkin' horse-sense now. Huccum yer done free?
Mr. Linkum tuk er pen an' writ down dese two lines
on de front leaf uv er blue-back spellin'-book, 'Niggers ez free fum ter-day out,' an' den he nail hit ter
de court-house do' up yonner in Washin'ton. An' fum
dat day tell now niggers ez been free ez anybody, an'
er heap freer dan po' white trash, which ef somebody
did n' own dey would starve ter deaf. What did
hit? I tell you what did hit; hit was de *pen!*" Here
the audience burst into applause.

"Huccum you niggers ain't starve ter deaf last year?
Huccum you had meal an' bread, hog an' hominy—an'

terbacco? I 'll tell yer erg'in! Yer go 'long up ter
Macon to de warehouse man an' tell him you mus'
have 'em. An' he say, 'Yer got er mule?' An' you
say, 'Oomhoo!' An' he ax you what 's es name; an'
you say, 'Scott; an' five years old.'" The speaker
smiled knowingly, and the crowd roared. "Den de
warehouse man say, 'Well, I put er mortgage on
Scott.' An' right dere he put de mortgage on Scott.
Den what nex'? Do dat man tell yer ter tech de
powdah? No, sah; he say tech de pen! Dat pen git
yo' rations fer er whole year. Hit 's de pen put de
mortgage on dat mule, an' s'port de whole county.
De mule git de mortgage, you git de rations, an' de
white man git left!" A wild cheer followed this
summary, and the old negroes ducked their heads,
and shook with emotion.

Friends of 'Lige began to eye him anxiously; but to
one who called out, "How 'bout dat, Unc' 'Lige?" he
only answered smilingly: "Give 'im rope! Give 'im
rope!"

Ike continued loudly: "What makes dat mortgage
stick? De law. What makes de law? De pen.
Dese hyah sheriffs and jedges an' lawyers go up yonner ter Atlanta an' git tergedder an' say: 'De people
want some new laws — mus' have some new laws.
De ole ones done all been broke.' An' dey set down
an' lay out some new laws. Does dey lay 'em out
wid powdah? No, sah; dey lay 'em out wid er pen.

"'Give 'im rope!!'"

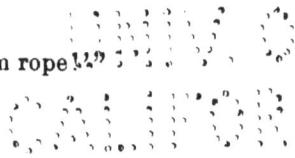

An' de jedge what 'force dem laws does hit wid er pen; an' de sheriff what come atter you fer swappin' dat mortgage mule come wid er paper what was writ wid er pen; an' de man what keep de jail he tek yer an' put yer name down in es book wid er pen; an' de fus' news yer git, bless Gord, de oberseer uv de chain-gang done got yer *in* er pen."

Shrieks of applause greeted this new point. When the confusion subsided, Uncle 'Lige said to Elder Hinson, who was at the far end of the room: "Br'er Peterson got er good memory fer hist'ry. Give 'im rope!" But Peterson was impervious.

"An' las' of all, my frien's, my dear frien's, how yer git dat Bible? Tell me dat. How yer git hit? De Lord mek Moses write hit on er stone. Now hyah ez er littl' 'screpancy, but in dem days pens was skearce, an' Moses was up on de mountain. So he des tek er chisel fer er pen, an' he whet hit on es boot, an' writ like de Lord say, usin' dat chisel fer er pen; an' right dere you got all de law an' de prophets. Oh, my dear frien's, powdah ez good, but de pen ez de mos' pow'ful. Powdah done knock down er heap er troof; but de troof what 's lef' ez de troof what uz write wid er pen. Dat 's all yer got ter swing ter ef yer ever 'spec' ter see de gates op'n when po' sinner knocks fer de las' time!"

Peterson sat down in triumph, and a bouncing girl brought him a big bouquet of dogwood-blossoms.

Intense silence greeted the rising of Elijah Williams. He straightened his portly form as well as he could, removed his spectacles, and began to smile. It was a little smile at first, but it spread with the rapidity of bad news, and very soon involved his whole face. It became an enormous, soundless laugh, and began to shake him from head to foot. The whole audience was infected, and the silence gave way to a round of fun. 'Lige looked at Peterson two or three times and made efforts to speak, but apparently could not. Presently the noise sank away, and the old man pronounced just one word :

"Pen-n-n !" It sounded like the bleat of a lost billy-goat, and was greeted with shouts of laughter.

"Huccum all you niggers hyah ?" he said, quoting his antagonist, and mimicking him. "Lemme tell you de troof, my frien's, an' you 'll know hit 's de troof ez soon ez you git hit. A white man sont er note fer you. Das right ! But did de note fetch you ? Did dat missionery pass hit erlong ter yer mammies and daddies ter read, an' did dey 'cep' of de white man's invertation, an' come erlong ? Not much ✛ Ain't one uv dem ole-time niggers ever seen writin' up ter dat time. Dey did n' know er pen fum a hump-back fiddle, an' dat 's er fac'. No, sir. I tell you how dey come. Dat ship-capt'n sail up by de bank, an' open up es pack. He spread out some speckle caliker on de san', an' op'n up er box er two

"Bouquet of dogwood-blossoms."

er snuff, an' fotch out some yaller beads, an' while dem niggers was 'miring dat speckle caliker, an' sneezin', an' fingerin' dem yaller-glass beads, de capt'n haul out er cannon full er powdah, an' shoot hit up in de air. An' right dere er hunderd niggers fell down proselyte to de groun', puffec'ly pluralyzed wid fear; an' he cotch 'em, an' slap 'em down in dat ship. Das how dey come hyah. Powdah fotch 'em." This magnificent rally on the part of their old leader roused the faithful to a frenzy of applause. The voice of 'Lige rang out over the clamor :

"An' dat writin' what Mr. Linkum nail up on de court-house do'. Was you niggers free fum dat day? No, sah. We had ter kill six hunderd million uv dem Yankees, an' dey had ter kill all our white folks, fus'; and hit took 'leven years ter do hit. Talk erbout de pen! Hit was de powdah sot you free.

"An' dat writin' what de sheriff come erlong an' fotch when he hunt dat mule you done swap — does de writin' fetch yer? Does yer stay in dat jail 'cause er de writin' en de book? Does yer stay on de chain-gang, workin' en de hot road, an' watermelons growin' right up ter side er de ditch, 'cause somebody totin' writin' erroun' en deir pockets? You know yer don't. Ain't no writin' en de worl' goin' ter hold air nigger in dis crowd under dat statement uv de case. You go 'long wid dat sheriff, an' yer go to dat jail, an' yer keep in de middl' er dat road, erway fum dem

melons, 'cause dere 's somebody erroun' totin' er gun
dat kin bark five times, fling er shell, and spit powdah
all over de face uv de yearth. Don't talk to me erbout
no pen. Hit ain't wurth er cent. Cow-pen, ink-pen,
or hog-pen — ef hit war n't fer de fac' dat er hog an'
de powdah could bofe beat er nigger to de swamp,
would n' er bin er pound er meat raised in Georgia las'
year.

"No, sah; don't talk erbout nobody's pen! Look
at Virge Williams when he met dat bear on de log
'cross Stone Creek las' week. What would de pen er
done fer Virge? S'pose Virge had took er pen out
uv es pocket, an' spit on de en' uv it, an' writ on dat
bear's face, 'Stop!' whar would Virge ha' been now?
Ef de powdah in dat gun had n' 'sploded when hit did,
an' kicked Virge out er de way er dat bear an' back
en de mud, whar we-all could prize 'm out wid er
fence-rail, I say, whar would Virge ha' been now?
Don't talk ter me erbout nobody's pen!

"Writin' ez mighty good an' writin' ez mighty
bad; but dis hyah techin' de pen so much ez what
keeps de country broke. Ef hit war n't fer dat pen
dere would n' be no mortgage, an' no jail, an' no
chain-gang. Rations would be boun' ter come any-
way, 'cause de cotton 'bleege ter come, an' hit teks er
nigger ter make cotton. An' powdah done spread
more gospel dan all de pens in de worl'. You got ter
have somebody ter 'splain er pen ter folks, but yer

"' Powdah 'splains hitself.'"

don't have ter 'splain de powdah. Powdah 'splains hitself. You got ter know er man 'fore you mind what es pen say; but you move fer anybody's powdah, whether yer know 'im er yer don't know 'im! Gimme powdah—gimme powdah—an' gi' Br'er Peterson er pen,—gi' 'im er gol' pen ef he wants hit,—an' ef I don't make 'im put down dat pen 'fo' he meks me put down dat powdah, den de pen ez mo' pow'ful dan de powdah."

'Lige closed amid such a storm of applause that no one thought it necessary to call for a vote.

CHARLEY AND THE POSSUM

I T was a day of great excitement in the court-room of the 2057th District, G. M. Charley Brood had been arrested for larceny, the particular charge being that he had stolen a possum and steel trap, the property of Peter Thompson. Charley having demanded that he be tried by a jury of his peers, the justice, with that accommodating spirit peculiar to some backwoods officers, had called in six colored gentlemen as a jury, arraigned the prisoner, and put the prosecutor under oath to tell the truth, the whole truth, and nothing but the truth. As Peter Thompson laid his aged lips upon the well-worn Bible, he rolled the white of his eyes into prominence, and let fall an ominous glance upon the prisoner at the bar, who had sunk down into his chair until the top of his shoulders was about level with his ears.

"Juedge, I tell yer how hit was," the witness began. "I drives er dray fer Marse Mansfiel', up en Macon, an' I works hard. I ain' got no time ter hunt up dere. I got er wife an' fambly ter tek cyah of. So when

I come down hyah ter my aunt's fun'al, I fotch erlong
er trap ter sot out, 'cause nigger 'bleege ter hab possum sometime. An' I sot hit out en de fur corner of
er corn-fiel' en de edge er de swamp, by er black-gum
tree, ter cotch er possum. I ain' got but fo' days
down hyah, juedge, an' I go ter dat trap ev'y mornin'
bout day, 'spectin' ter fin' er possum dere ter tek home
ter my wife an' fambly. Las', one mornin', I go dere,
an' I see possum signs all ober der place. I say:
'Peter, bless goodness, dat sho' big bo' possum.' Den
I say 'g'in: 'Huh! dat strong possum. Done tote
trap off.' But I knowed 'e ain' tote hit fur; an' I 'gin
ter look erbout. I look, an' I look, an' I look! Ain'
see no possum nowhar! Den bimeby I see nigger
track; an' 'bout dat time I know wha' de matter. I
was sho' mad. I des tek dat trail like er houn' dog.
Juedge, ef I had er cotch dat nigger *den*, I would n'
er be'n hyah now, an' he would n', nuther. I 'd er kill
'im right dere!

"Well, suh, I run t'rough dem fiel's like er man's
tracks; las' I struck de railroad. I look dis way an'
I look dat way, an' den I saw dis hyah nigger wid er
bag on es shoulder, 'way down de railroad. Fus'
news he know, I was dere. I sez, sez I: 'Mornin',
Charley,' — des so.

"An' he say: 'Mornin'.'

"'How you do?' sez I.

"'I 'm toler'ble,' sez 'e. 'How you do?'

"An' I up an' say: 'I'm toler'ble.'

"He don' say no more, an' bimeby I up an' come erg'in:

"'What you got en dat bag, Charley?'

"Den 'e say:

"'Unc' Peter, I so tired. Bin 'way down ter de station ter git my wife some 'taters. She mighty sick an' hank'rin' atter 'taters, an' our 'taters all got de dry-rot.'

"He ain' answer de question, juedge, an' I gi' hit ter 'im erg'in. Sez I:

"'What yer got en dat bag, Charley?'

"Den 'e say: 'Hit 's er long way ter de station, an' ef my wife had n' bin sick she 'd ha' ter done 'thout 'taters.'

"Juedge, 'e ain' say 'taters en de bag — des keep on talkin' roun' 'bout es sick wife an' bein' tired. Den I wanter see how big er liar de nigger kin be, an' I ax de question erg'in. 'Bout dat time, while he was studyin' up er new lie, I see de possum twist en de bag, an' right dere I re'ch out my han' an' grab de bag fum 'im an' shuk hit, 'cause I was determ' ter see what en dat bag. He ain' try ter hender me, an' he better not, 'cause, ef 'e had, dere 'd er bin er rookus right dere. Well, juedge, I shuk, an' I shuk, an' I shuk, but nothin' drap. An' den I say:

"'Charley, look like dem 'taters mus' hab toofs an' toe-nails ter hol' on wid.' An' I shuk erg'in.

"' Charley,' sez I, des so, 'mebbe dem 'taters got de tail wrapped roun' er knot en de bag'; an' wi' dat I turn hit wrong side out, an' down drap de possum wid he foot en de trap, an' de lyin' nigger throw up bofe han's an' say:

"' Lordy-mussy, what dat possum gwine do wid dat trap!'

"Juedge, I done eat dat possum; hyah he foot en de trap, hyah de trap, an' dere de nigger. He ain' done me right, no, 'e ain'."

There was silence for a few moments. Fingal Cave Scotland, the oldest man on the jury, bent his gray head down close to the ear of Ubadiah Lafayette and whispered solemnly. The face of the Rev. Septimus Smith, who sat at the other end of the jury, was grave. Others exchanged comments. Evidently it was a threatening moment for Charley; but Charley came to the stand smilingly.

"Hit 's des lak dis, juedge," he began. "I ain' no town nigger, an' I 'm proud er de troof. I ain' so triflin' I cyan't git work whar I was borned an' ha' ter run ter town. An' I 'm proud er de troof erg'in. Dese hyah town niggers,"— and all eyes were directed toward the late witness,— "dey 'low as how dey own de whole worl' an' ev'rythin' dat wears hair er feathers fum hen-roos' ter possum-holler. Dey ain' satisfy en town; dey mus' come down hyah an' bre'k up de ole-time huntin' an' fishin' wi' dey trapsions an' dey nets.

Ef dey 'd come lak er white man an' hunt wi' er dog
an' er gun, hit 'd er bin diff'unt, an' folks 'd had some
'spec' fer 'em. Ain' dat so, Unc' Finger ? "

This appeal to the prejudices of the country negro
had an immediate effect upon the jury.

" Hit sho' ez de troof," replied Fingal; and his companions seemed to coincide with him. The prisoner
continued:

" Juedge, I sorter like possum merse'f, but I ain'
sot no trap. I hunt 'im wid de dog an' de torch, lak
er man. Dat night I was out tryin' ter show er fool
puppy how ter trail, an' bimeby he opened up an' lit
out. I sez ter merse'f: 'Charley, you gwine ter hab
possum fer dinner.' An' 'bout dat time I des natchully
laugh out loud. 'You gwine ter hab barbecue possum,' sez I. Juedge, I see dat possum right 'fo' me
en de dish, brown all ober."

A slight shudder shook the form of the Rev. Septimus Smith, and a momentary sensation swayed the
other jurymen. It was as a little breeze wandering
in among sleepy rushes.

" I seed dem split sweet 'taters roun' dat possum
lak er yaller-hawberry chain roun' er nigger gal's
neck. I seed de brown gravy leakin' down es sides
as 'e lay dere cryin' fer joy all ober, an' er jug er 'sim-
mon beer — "

" Hyah ! hyah ! hyah ! hyah-h-h-h ! Hyah ! hyah !
hyah ! Hoo-ee-e ! "

This explosion came from Fingal Cave Scotland, who doubled up, and would have fallen out of the chair but for the restraining hand of his next neighbor. The sensation was complete; the little breeze had become a whirlwind.

The court administered a ponderous rebuke, and the witness proceeded :

"Hit was des dat way, juedge ; an' I hope yo' Honor ain' think hard er Unc' Finger fer his natchul feelin's, 'cause las' possum I taste, hit war fixed up an' on es table lak I tell yer. An' dey 'd be dere more oftener ef hit war n' fer dese hyah biggitty town niggers an' dey traps."

"Go on with your story." The judge rapped the table with his knuckles.

"Yessah. Well, juedge, by dat time de fool puppy plum' out er hearin', an' I knowed he done struck er fox. Hit was de July blood en 'im. I 'gin ter look roun' fer home, 'cause day breakin', when I stumble on somep'n', an', bless Gord, dere was de possum settin' right 'fo' me. I sez : 'Charley, hyah possum de Lord sont yer.' Possum he settin' up dere by esse'f, an' eyes des er-shinin'. I sez : 'Huh! dis possum he sick! No, possum ain' sick ; he des too fat ter trabbel. I sho' eat dis possum.' Den I look erg'in. Dah, now ! Possum hitch en er trap ! I say ter merse'f, ' Charley, dis ain' yo' possum : dis somebody else's possum ! You ain' gwine tek 'n'er man's possum, is yer ?' Den

I say: 'No, course I ain' gwine tek dis hyah possum! What I want wid 'n'er man's possum?' an' walk right off, sorter singin' ter merse'f: 'Raccoon tail am ringed all roun'.'

"I git 'bout fifteen foot erway, an' den I kinder natchully look back, an', juedge, hit 's Gord's troof, dat littl' ole possum settin' back dere on dat trap look so col' an' shiv'rin', I feel sorry fer 'im — settin' back dere, 'way out en de wet swamp, so col' an' lonesome, an' de owls des er-hollerin' an' de heel-taps er-hammerin' up en de dead trees. I sez ter merse'f: 'Charley, you sho' ain' gwine lef' dat po' littl' possum out hyah all by esse'f en de big swamp, ez yer? Somep'n' boun' ter cotch 'im, sho'.' Den I sez: 'Who 'e b'long ter, anyhow? Did de man wha' sot dat trap raise 'im? Does dat man own dis hyah lan'? Does 'e own de holler tree dis hyah po' littl' wand'rin' possum born en? No, 'e don',' sez I. 'Possum is es own boss.' Den I go back an' look 'im en de eye, an' I say: 'Littl' possum, you col', ain' yer?' An', bless goodness, he smile cl'ar back twell es jaw-toof shine. An' I sez: 'Does yer wanter git en Charley's warm-bag an' go 'long back ter sleep?' An' 'e smile erg'in. An' I sez: 'All right, but how 'bout dat trap?' An', juedge, den dat possum look se'ious, an' lay es nose down on es leg. I tell 'im den: 'Littl' possum, Charley ain' gwine lef' yer out hyah en de col', an' you bin up all night. He gwine ter drap yer en de bag,

'cause you yo' own boss an' kin come an' go, but ef
you fetch dat trap erlong, hit 's yo' own 'sponsibleness.
Charley ain' got no business ter tech 'n'er man's trap.
But I gwine shet bofe eyes, an' dere won' be no
witnuss.'

" Den de possum he smile erway back erg'in, an' I
drap 'im en de bag, bofe eyes shet.   An', juedge, dat 's
de Lord's troof.   I ain' tech dat trap.   Dere hit ez
down dere on de flo', wi' de possum han' still on hit.
I ain' git er smell er dat possum, an' I ain' stole
nothin'! "

There was a murmur of applause as Charley concluded, but this was quickly repressed.   The justice,
putting on his glasses, read the law as to wild animals to the jury, and explained what was meant by
larceny; and the jury retired.   When they returned,
they brought in a verdict of " not guilty."   This was
explained afterward by the Rev. Septimus Smith.   He
said that the jury was clearly of the opinion that a
possum was no man's property until actually in his
possession, and that if the trap was stolen, it had
been stolen by the possum, and not by Charley Brood.